Life outside the Boat

"WALKING ON WATER"

"Life Outside the Boat"

All Scripture quotations, unless indicated, are taken from the New American Standard Bible,

Published by:
Ransom Ministries Inc.
Mobile, Al 36685

This book is dedicated to my My Wife Tara for all her support and love through this process and her consistently seeking God for our family I will always be thankful to God for bringing us together at just the right time and also my 5 girls Teagan, Shelby, Abbey, Miceala,
and Mary Paige
we will all be together ONE DAY!!

Contents

Acknowledgments

I want to thank each and every church that has partnered with us in this process and all the supporters of this mission.

WE CAN'T WAIT TO SEE WHAT GOD IS GOING TO DO IN THE FUTURE.

I also want to thank my family for believing in us enough not to voice how crazy they thought this whole thing was even though they were thinking that we had lost our minds.

Introduction

No matter who you are or what you do, relationships are an important part of that. We come in contact with so many people in any given day that can affect our lives in dramatic ways and we don't even realize it. Early in 2010, God started to really move on my wife, Tara, and I that we needed to step out in faith and completely surrender to His will for our lives. We attended a bible study at our church called "If You Want to Walk on Water, You've Got to Get Out of the Boat," by John Ortberg. We began praying and asking God to show us what "walking on water" looked like for us and how we could use the gifts He had given us to bring glory to Him. During this time God reveled to me that I need to let go of some things in order to walk on the water He was setting before us. This was one of the hardest things I had ever done but I trusted Him to do what He promised to do. Then God started to reveal to me a vision of a cafe where anyone could get a hot meal and pay whatever they could afford. God placed the word "ransom" and the scripture, Matthew 20:28, "For the Son of Man came not to be served, but to serve and to give his life as a ransom for many" into Tara's heart. When we began to dissect this verse, we discovered the Greek word that is translated "to serve" actually meant "one that waits on tables," and "ransom" meant "to liberate many from misery." This scripture confirmed in both of us that we were

to allow Christ to work through our serving tables to liberate many from misery through relationship with us, but ultimately through relationship with Him.
Over the next few months, God did some amazing things. He opened doors only He could open (You'll learn more of the details in the first chapter.) and on October 28, 2010 Ransom Ministries began with our first location of Ransom Café, an eatery in a local church where we offered a hot fresh lunch for whatever someone could donate whether it be money or time. Since then, God has added more projects to Ransom. We have the Clean Machine, a 22 foot shower and laundry trailer we use to serve the homeless and others in need. We host Youth mission camps, and operate Ransom ReProgram, a job skills training program utilizing the Jobs for Life Curriculum encouraging people to match their employment with their God-given gifts and talents so they can experience the abundant life God promised us.

Through the last 7 years we have seen and heard some of the most unbelievable stories of perseverance and victory, but also of heartbreak and hopelessness. In the process we have learned what we have done wrong and what we have done right in building relationships with others. We have learned how important healthy relationships are in the kingdom of God. He created us to be in relationship with Him, with others, and with the world around us.

My prayer for you is as you read; you will be challenged to look at yourself and others differently. We all have frequent opportunities to form genuine, healthy relationships with people different than us. God, help us all to see them. May your eyes be opened as you journey through these pages. At times you could want to close your eyes and look away, but hang with it, and keep your eyes and heart open. Your next best friend might just be waiting for someone to care enough to offer a Mercy and Justice balanced relationship. To live the abundant life God promised, you must allow God to lead you into what He has created you for; relationships.

~Matt Armbruster

CHAPTER 1

(TRUST)

It all started at Jubilee Baptist Church in Daphne, Alabama with a Bible Study called "If You Want to Walk on Water, You've Got to Get Out of the Boat," by John Ortberg. My wife, Tara, and I learned through that study, in order to see miracles, you have to take the first step out of your boat. Once you've stepped out, stay focused. Over time and through much prayer, we started to ease our feet over the edge of our boat. Then came a face to face meeting with God that took me by surprise and my life has been forever changed. The men at our church were planning to attend a Christian Men's Conference at another local church and several of my friends ask me to go with them. My first response was, "No way!" I had been hurt by "Christians" and I had a problem with trust and not just with people. It was hard, really hard, for me to trust God. I had been hurt, betrayed, and lied to by people I was closest to and I didn't understand why God would allow this to happen to me when I was doing my best to live for Him. At this point in my life, I really didn't want to be around a bunch of men, especially Christian men. Tara and I had been married several years and I had forgiven those people that had hurt me. I had seen how God used that situation for my good, but there was still a struggle going on inside me and I had mostly been playing church. Tara told me she thought I really needed to go to the conference, so I gave in and went. Men, our wives usually know what is best for us before we do, so we really should listen to them more. Even though I didn't want to be there and I had set in my mind I was not getting anything out of this weekend, during the conference the speaker for the event, Rick Burgess, shared his testimony. His three year old son had drowned while he was out of town on a speaking engagement. He said the Lord spoke to him as he prayed on the plane ride home. He asked God the same question I had about what I went through and the same question that many of us find ourselves asking God when we go through difficult times in our lives; "Why?" He said God responded to him by telling him that he could do one of two things, he could either blame God for what happened, or he could see how God would be glorified through it. At that moment, I came face to face with the reality that I had been blaming God for something that was not His fault. I was completely broken in that moment. I cried out to God and confessed my mistrust and the years of doubt. I told Him I would do whatever He asked me to do. I had given my life to Christ in April of 1996, my day of salvation, but this was my day of consecration.

Well, I admit I had no idea what that meant at the time, but over the next few months God started to reveal to me part of His plan as I began to place my complete trust in Him and get out of the boat. God gave me an idea of a restaurant where people could come eat and order off a menu with no prices on it. Customers would donate what they could afford or if they could not contribute financially, they could donate their time in the way of serving in the restaurant. I had spent many years managing restaurants and even owned one. Restaurant life is tough. It's not always easy to make a restaurant profitable and I knew this was a terrible business plan. I went round and round with God about this and each time He would remind me "You did say anything I asked, right?"

At this point I hadn't shared this vision with Tara. When we got married, we had decided restaurant life was not conducive to families with small children. We sold the restaurant and left that life behind when we got married. I wasn't sure how she would receive the idea of jumping back into that world even though the girls were a little older now.

Tara and I both knew that we needed to get our personal finances in a better place to be able to do whatever God was calling us to. We began to pray, plan, and prepare. We both had good jobs and were mostly happy with our employment. One day, I was driving home from work and a man I had never met called me and offered me a job. This job was all the way in Moses Lake, Washington. We lived in Daphne, AL. He needed someone to be the Quality Control Manager for an electrical company and they were willing to pay a salary I had only dreamed of. I was really not even qualified to do this job by any stretch of the imagination. I had worked at a Chevron plant in Mississippi for a few months, but actually had very little experience with this type work. I told him, "Thanks, but no thanks. I can't leave home for that long." I went home and told Tara about this crazy call I had received and she said "How do you not know that this job isn't part of God's plan?" Remember guys, listen to your wives. They are the smart ones. At least, that was the case in my situation. Well, I went to call the man back to get some more information and before I could, he called me and said "I'm a man of God and you need to have this job." He had my attention. I will remind you I had not applied for this job or sent them a resume. My curiosity got the best of me, so I asked him where he got my name and contact information. He told me that he and the quality control guy at the plant in Moses Lake were walking through the plant talking about their need for a Quality Control Manager for this job and how the position needed to be filled as soon as possible. While they were having this conversation, they walked past another man that was working in the plant. He stopped them and asked what position they were looking to fill? They told him and he said he knew a guy that he had worked with at a Chevron plant in Pascagoula, Mississippi that would be a good fit. So he gave me your name and phone number, so I called you.

That story was just too unexplainable to deny the hand of God in it. Like I said previously, I had worked at the Chevron plant for a very short time and my position there was just a file clerk. Every now and then I would go out and look at the job with the Quality Control Manager, but I had never actually done that job. Plus if you've never been in a plant like that, they are very loud and noisy. A lot of the guys wear ear plugs in the plant. But, this one guy in that plant across the United States from where we worked together just happened to overhear this conversation. I know that God was organizing this all behind the scenes, even the job in Mississippi, for this moment in my life. Well, we talked through the details of my salary and I was amazed that they would pay me so much to do this job, but I knew it was going to take a lot to be able to tackle the path God had set before us and this was obviously a part of His provision. I left for Moses Lake, Washington on Easter Sunday in 2010 and worked there for 6 months. I was able to spend a lot of time in God's word and in prayer seeking His plan for our future. I learned in my time there, that having an IDEA is great, but when opposition comes, you put that idea on the back burner. When you have a BURDEN for something that is great as well, but the first time something doesn't go the way you thought it should you get discouraged and stop. But if you have a PASSION for something, nothing (I mean, nothing!) or nobody will ever cause you to give up.

For example, if you have an IDEA that you want to go live in the streets to bring awareness to homelessness, on that first night when it starts raining and gets cold, you will probably think this might not have been such a good idea and quit. Maybe you have a BURDEN for the homeless so you decide to go out and give away some clothes, food, or something else. When a few of the homeless people start being ugly or worse they cuss you out because you don't have their size clothes or they're tired of peanut butter crackers, then you get upset and discouraged and decide not to go back. But, if you have a PASSION for helping others nothing will change your mind. You will get discouraged and want to quit during tough times, but the passion burning inside you won't let you quit. There will be times you feel like it's all a waste of time and nothing your doing is making a difference, but the passion inside you won't let you quit. Over the six months I spent in Moses Lake, God put in me a passion to help people realize their God-given abilities and to help them develop into who God intended them to be. That passion started to burn inside me like I never thought possible. Over those six months, God gave me the ability to do the job set before me and do it with excellence. I couldn't and still can't take any credit for the job I did at that plant in Washington. I know it was the power of Christ working through me that gave me the ability to do a job that I was not qualified to do.

Occasionally, I would fly home for the weekend to see my family. One of my first trips back was for Abbey and Mary Paige's dance recital. We had a great time together as a family that weekend and I decided it would be a good time to tell Tara about the restaurant vision God had given me. I had been to Tara with a couple of different ideas, because I'm the idea guy and she's my logistics lady or as she likes to say, I'm the gas and she's the brakes. I really wasn't sure how this was going to go over, but when I began telling her, she started smiling. At first, I thought she was going to laugh at me, but to my surprise, she said she thought that was it. God had been impressing in her the word "Ransom" and the scripture Matthew 20:28, "the Son of Man did not come to be served, but to serve and give his life as a ransom for many." When we began to dissect this verse, we discovered the Greek word that is translated "to serve" actually meant "one that waits on tables," and "ransom" meant "to liberate many from misery." This confirmed in both of us that we were to allow Christ to work through our serving tables to liberate many from misery through relationship with us, but ultimately with Him. We decided to name the restaurant ministry, Ransom Café.

I will admit it was very tempting to go onto another job with that company when the Moses Lake project was complete. Did I tell you about the money? By the world's standards, I could have been very successful if I continued to work for them, but I knew it would not be good if I went against what God was calling us to do. Remember it was never my ability to do the job. It was His power that allowed me to do the job. Tara flew out to Seattle and we started our drive back to Daphne on September 1, 2010. It was a great time for us to discuss our ideas and talk through the plans to begin the ministry. It was so good for us to spend some quality time together after being apart.

When we returned the real work began. We had lots of questions; where would we do this? , how would it work? what would the menu be? All those questions and many more kept coming up. I set up a meeting with a guy that ran a restaurant in a church in Mobile that used the money to fund their mission, Mars Hill Café. We sat down and I told him my idea. He said, "I know the perfect place to do that. I think it's called the Hangar. It's part of West Mobile Baptist church on Airport Blvd. I'm not sure if they would let you use it, but it's worth a try". When he said that, he didn't know that when I left there, I was already scheduled to meet with Bro. Charles Gibbs, the pastor of West Mobile Baptist Church. You see, Bro. Charles was the same pastor that preached the message on Easter Sunday in 1996, the day I gave my life to Jesus. He was a mentor of mine and a person I trusted to give me sound advice. Another thing I should mention to you is about 10 years before while I was a member of the church, I helped the youth pastor design and layout the kitchen in the Hangar at the time the church was building it for their student ministry. Well, I finished my meeting at Mars Hill and headed to my meeting with Brother Charles Gibbs. We sat down and I unfolded my idea and vision. I fully expected Charles to say he would be praying for me because to be honest I had come to him with some pretty crazy ideas in the past. He listened to me and then to my surprise he asked me if the Hangar would work for that. I almost fell out of my chair! But I held it together and just said I thought it would. This began the drive forward to open the first Ransom Café in the Hangar of WMBC. We now had a place and we had settled on a menu of pizza, soup and sandwiches. We were ready to move forward. These meetings happened in September of 2010 and on October 28, 2010, we served our first plate of food and have been doing it ever since.

What is God telling you to do or what is God gifted you with? Will you do it and trust He will work out the details? Trust is a tough thing especially if people have let you down your whole life. Trusting people you can see is hard so trusting someone you cannot see or touch is even harder than trusting a person at times. As you move into this walk of serving you first have to work on you trusting God yourself that He is in control. You then can move on to trusting others and being ok with them when they don't act exactly like you think they should. Throughout the book I hope you can trust and see that God is in control and we sometimes have to step out of the boat by faith in order to see all He has for us. Just Keep Reading He paid the Ransom for you all you need to do is except it by faith.

CHAPTER 2

(FAITH)

Cheese, Broken floors, and Angels

The day we opened, I think we served around 30 people and to sit back and watch it unfold was the most amazing thing I think I ever witnessed. Things ran so smoothly, it could only be explained by a move of God. We started out with very little capital; ok no capital to speak of. This was a total faith thing without really knowing what each day would bring, just the peace that God was in it.

Not long after we had opened, I was getting things ready for the day when I noticed we had run out of cheese. Remember our menu was Pizza, soup, sandwiches, and salad. I don't know about you, but I've never had a pizza without cheese and I start thinking it would not be a good thing. Well, I didn't have time to go get some cheese or really the funds to and I was the only one there. I did the only thing I knew to do. I got down on my knees in the middle of the kitchen and began to pray and ask God to provide us some cheese. I know you're thinking that seems a little trivial and if I'm honest, in that moment I knew it was trivial. I also knew that if this was going to work, we needed to depend on God for everything. As I finished my prayer, I heard a knock on the back door. I answered it and there stood a good friend of mine, Mario, who runs a local restaurant in town. He stood there holding 3 five pound bags of shredded cheese. He told me one of his employees had ordered the wrong cheese and he just felt like he was supposed to bring it to me instead of sending it back. He didn't know why, but he did what he felt like he was supposed to do. I stood there, holding that cheese with tears in my eyes and Mario looking at me like I was crazy until I told him I had just prayed for God to send me some cheese and God used him to answer my prayer. God also used that cheese to remind me He controls everything, even cheese. I know you may be thinking, really?! God really cares about cheese?! He's God! But, I am here to tell you He does. He cares about EVERY detail of your life; all of your unimportant to you stuff matter to God.

On another day while I was getting ready to open the café, I heard a knock on the back door. I opened it to find a young lady with two small kids. The lady was crying. I invited them in and she began telling me her story. Her kids were getting ready for school and while they were standing in the bathroom, the floor gave way and the kids fell through it. She said they could not live in this place one more day. The landlord would not fix anything and would not even listen to her concerns. She said that her husband had a job in Tennessee where they had family and if they could just make it there, they would have a place to stay and he would have a job. I asked her how much it would take to get there and she said about $100 in fuel and that is all they needed. I told her I would see what I could do. I don't give out money to people very often without getting to know them first. Our mantra from the beginning was a hand up and not a hand out we want to partner with people in their lives. I had her give me their number and I told her I would get in touch with her. She was very sincere and I believed what she was telling me. I was praying through what God would have us do and I checked our ministry bank account. We had $128.00 in the account and it was only Wednesday. We were so new and funds were so tight, I would purchase food supplies one day at a time. I still had to buy food for two more days. I put it out on social media that we had a family in need and asked if anyone could help. A few people messaged me and said they could help next week. I felt God speak to my spirit that they needed to get out of that situation now. He reminded me we had the $100 to give them. So, I began to argue with God which is not a good idea if you have ever done it you know what I mean. I thought I had some valid points, but I just kept hearing God ask, "Do you trust me?" Well I decided I would go to Walgreens and get some gift cards for them when I got there I picked out three Shell Oil $25 gift cards and proceeded to the check out, when I felt God nudge me. "Didn't they say $100?" And again I began to argue, "At least I'm doing something!" and He put these words in my head, "But, not what I told you to do." So I headed back to the rack with the gift cards on it and reluctantly picked up another $25 gas card and then I heard, "You know they will need to feed those kids on the way, so why not get them a Subway card, too. $25 should be enough to feed the family of four." By now I am getting real unhappy with this voice in my head and I am thinking how we only have $128 and if I spend $125, I'll only have $3.00. We can't make it for two days on $3.00 and I'm trying to start a new ministry! Well, I picked up the Subway gift card and headed to the checkout stand again over the years I have learned it does no good to argue with God. I purchased all of the cards and headed back to the café. I walk in the door and one of the volunteers told me we were out of bleach and we needed to sanitize the dishes. I just about lost it to be honest I stormed out the door and went back and bought a bottle of bleach which cost $1.50 with tax and went back to the café. If I'm honest, I was pretty irritated. I started questioning why I was doing this and thinking I should've kept being a Quality Control Manager. If you passed 1st grade math, you know I had less than $1.50 left in our account. I was really stressed to say the least. I called the lady and asked her to bring her family back to the café. I had something for her. She showed up about 20 minutes later and I gave her the cards. She looked at them with tears in her eyes and said you will never know what this means to me and my family. I would like to tell you it felt so good to help them and I was happy for this family, but to be honest I was still stressed and all I could think was "so what now?! Lord, what now?!" I truly thought this was the end of Ransom as we knew it. I limped through the day and one of our regulars came in to eat. I sat down and began talking with him. This guy, who I'll refer to as Bob, had been very open about his lack of faith. He claimed to be an atheist and he knew I was a Christian and I had previously shared with him our whole purpose in starting the café. As we talked that day, I felt like I was supposed to tell him the story about the lady and her family. At first, I really had made up my mind not to, but the more we talked the more I couldn't shake that feeling. So I began to tell Bob the story. I may have left out some of details about my pity party and arguing with God, but I was completely honest about our lack of funds. I came to the happy ending and I said something that even surprised me. I said "I don't know how God is going to provide, but I know He will. He has never let me down before and He won't start now." It was time to close up and Bob asked me for a ride home and I told him I could take him. I decided to swing by the mailbox on our way. I don't know why. We very seldom had anything in there anyway, but it was on the way so I stopped. I looked inside and there were 3 envelopes. I took the mail to the car and I began to open them. Remember my friend, Bob, is in the passenger seat watching me. I open the first envelope and there's a check for $200. I opened the 2nd and inside it was a check for $225 and I open the last one and it's a check for $275!! I sat there staring at them and tears started to run down my face and I heard God's voice again in my head "Now do you trust me"? I looked over to my friend, Bob, and said "There is no other explanation for this, but God!" He looked at me and all he could say is "WOW!" I did a lot of praying and asking God to forgive me for my unbelief that night. I knew God had forgiven me, but I also knew this probably wouldn't be the last time I didn't trust Him. He spoke into my heart that night and told me when you start to struggle with trusting me again, just remember this day. Choose trust.

We were about 2 years into this journey and again things were tight in the area of finances. It seemed like that is where we struggled the most because that was an area it was the hardest for me to trust Him so He kept having to give me opportunities to practice trust. I was fretting about how we were going to make it when a good friend of mine walked in and said I came by to pray for you today. I sure needed it. He began to pray and said something like this "Lord, You know what Matt needs and you are the only one that can give it to him. God, I pray that people will come off the street by your drawing and sow into this ministry. Please Lord; show yourself strong on Matt's behalf. Amen." I thanked him and we talked a while about family and how things were going with him and he went on his way. Later that day, we had closed up and it was just me cleaning up things. I had locked the doors and was getting ready to leave when I noticed a young man pull up to the front door on his bike. He had a backpack on and my first thought was he was a homeless guy looking for help. I really didn't want to deal with it, but there was that voice again. So I went and opened the door and asked him if I could help him. He asked me if this was Ransom Café and I told him it was. He walked over to his backpack that was hanging on his bike and pulled out a piece of paper and began to write on it. He came back over to me and handed me the paper. He said the Lord told me to give you this and he got on his bike and rode off. I looked down at the paper and it was a money order with a scripture reference written on it. *"I will save you; you will not fall by the sword but will escape with your life, because you trust in me, declares the Lord." (Jeremiah 39:18)* The money order was for $208. That was the start of this young man coming by every month for 2 years on his bike giving what he had. Each time it was a money order with a scripture reference. We couldn't read his name on the signature of the first money order, so we began to refer to him as our bicycle angel. We now know his name and occasionally still hear from him. We have no doubt he was sent to us by God.

As you can see from these 3 stories, even when we are not the most faithful, He is. Even when our faith is weak, He gives us grace. One thing I have learned over the years is my human nature tends to doubt and not trust, but if I can just remember- God is in control. I would like to tell you I trust and obey each and every time now without arguing or doubting, but that would not be true. However, each time I do trust Him, I see His power. Whether it comes through financial blessing, spiritual blessings, or even cheese, God comes through and it does get easier to have faith in Him.

I have also found that serving others is a lot like golf. You go out on the course and hit some bad shots and think what in the world am I doing out here. I am terrible and this just frustrates me. It's a complete waste of my time. Then you swing and hit one or two balls perfectly and you think to yourself this game isn't so bad. With a little practice, I could be pretty good at this. Serving others can be frustrating and make you wonder why you are wasting your time doing this. Then that one guy or girl comes along and gets it. They understand who they are in Christ and see who they can be. They take the effort to move forward and allow you to walk with them through the roadblocks that get in their way. Feels like a 300 yard drive straight down the fairway, but much more rewarding.

So what are you struggling to trust God by faith with? What decision do you need to turn over to Him? What need should you give to Him? Today is the day to turn it all over to him whether it is financial, physical, or spiritual He wants you to have faith that He is in control and really you have nothing to lose so take the step in faith and surrender your will and desires to Him. The only way to see God's Miracles and power are to give him the controls and have faith that He will come through.

CHAPTER 3

(UNDERSTANDING)

Are You Kidding Me, Lord?

Over the course of a few months, I was getting a strong feeling that I really didn't know what the people we served actually went through on a daily basis. While I had people generously give to me during the divorce and my greatest times of need, I had never been homeless or dealt with the things they many of our patrons were navigating. So as I prayed that day I felt God nudging me to go homeless on purpose for a period of time. I said, and I think it was out loud, "ARE YOU KIDDING ME, LORD?!" That is the last thing I wanted to do, so I pushed that thought aside and went about my day. I was thinking I could read a book or learn from the people coming in to the café, going homeless was a little extreme. The next few weeks I didn't even pray much because I was afraid I would feel His push toward this project, again. Eventually, I went to Tara, my wife, and told her what I felt I was being led to do. Since she was usually the brakes, I thought she would shoot down the idea, but to my surprise she agreed with God and not me. I wasn't surprised that she disagreed with me, but why did she have to do it this time when I was looking for an out?! Well, we both started praying about how my being homeless looked and would be accomplished. During this time, God had sent a man who I'll call George, to the café. George was homeless, but he liked the idea of being able to provide his own meal by volunteering in the café. George would come every day and worked hard. He quickly became more than a volunteer. He was a great friend and someone that I trusted to keep things going if I couldn't be there. George told me that the first day he came into the Ransom Café; He had really given up hope and something told him to stop at the café and there he found not only a good meal, but good people looking to form relationships and make new friends. He found hope and realized that God had sent him there that day. But God didn't send him just for him. He sent George there to teach me a few things and the first lesson I learned from him was that I had no idea what people that lived on the streets went through and why it was hard for them to go to church or just get a job like a lot of people are quick to suggest. He talked to me about what he went through on a daily basis and he encouraged me to experience it if just for a little while so I could better understand.

Mardi gras weekend seemed like the best possible time for my homeless experiment, so we put it on the calendar. Over the next few weeks leading up to this day I tried to rationalize not doing it and told God all of the reasons it was not a good idea. I talked at length with George about his experiences and got a lot of great advice from him. As it got closer to time for me to go homeless, I began to get a peace about it and I started to pray that God would teach me so and change the way I looked at others through this adventure. As you read in detail the actual account of the three day journey excerpt from our "Walking on Water" blog, my prayer for you is that as you read it, God will change the way you look at and act towards those in need, the way He did for me.

Walking on Water (*February 2012*)

Day 1:

I started with a backpack, tent, sleeping bag, books, and a change of clothes, a protein bar, flashlight, $10 cash, and the clothes on my back. It was Saturday, February 19, and I was still hoping God would change His mind and tell me I really didn't have to do this.

I parked my car at the cafe at 7:30 a.m. and began to walk. Thank God there was a break in the rain. I had decided where I was going to put my tent, so I started walking there. It rained off and on all the way, and I had to duck into McDonalds one time when the rain got real heavy. After it let up, I walked a few more blocks and I got to the location I thought I would stay at around 9:30 a.m. It was raining a little harder then, so I darted in the woods to get to my spot.

As I am walking in I noticed two people leaning against a tree covered by a blue tarp. I walked slowly, trying to make some noise so I wouldn't startle them. I talked with them a while and did not get a good feeling about them, so I prayed with them and moved on. I walked up to a bus stop cover and sat under there for about an hour while it poured down rain. I didn't know what I was going to do except walk and try to find another place. Once the rain let up a little, I began to walk, really not knowing where I was going to tell the truth — just wandering without a real plan, and for me, that was difficult. I walked and walked and along the way checked wooded areas as I came to them to see if there was a good spot, and each time there were either signs of someone staying in the woods or there actually was someone.

You really don't want to stay in a place with others, because to be honest, you do the same thing in the woods that most people do in their homes. (Wash up, use the restroom, etc.) And if you don't like people walking up on you in your home, so it goes in the woods. I kept walking and looking, feeling a little more desperate as I went. It really started to rain so I got under an overhang at a church to get out of it. By now everything is soaked — my clothes, backpack, what was inside the backpack — so I just sat there, frustrated, cold, and really wanting to stop this. I sat there and someone drove up. They saw me and immediately backed up and left. I continued to walk again after the rain let up a little. It is around 12 p.m., so it had only been a few hours, but I can tell you it seemed like much longer.

I checked a couple more wooded areas, but again, each time there were people in them trying to stay dry. About 2:30, I found a place to set up my tent that looked good and could not be seen from anyone on the road or walking around. I set the tent up in the rain and had a hard time keeping the inside dry as I did it. I was done setting up around 3:30, and I got inside and sat there, wondering if it would ever stop raining. I then realized I had no water or food to eat, so I began to hope the rain would stop so I could get out and get some water at the very least. Finally it let up, so I unloaded my backpack of all the wet stuff so I would have something to carry the water in. I went to the gas station and had to buy a gallon jug of water and then I went to the laundromat to see if they would let me charge my phone, and they did! Well, I sat there and then the bottom fell out. It began to rain so hard I could not see the light pole in the parking lot. I began to wonder what was happening to my tent and how I was going to get back before dark because I had forgot my flashlight.

I sat there until about 5:30 and realized that it wasn't going to stop, so I begin to walk. I went into the woods and the path that I had taken was 6 inches under water, so I waded back, thinking my tent was probably soaked through. When I got there, it was fine, and I got inside and tried to figure out if I had anything dry. I didn't, except my sleeping bag, a t-

shirt and a pair of underwear that I had in a waterproof bag — thank God. Well I got into my sleeping bag at 6:15 and realized it was 12 hours until daylight, and I'm in a tent with lightning storms and tornado watches going on. As hard as it is for me to admit, I was scared and wanted to go home. But then I thought of those who don't have a place to go home to, and I prayed for them and it took my focus off of me. I pulled out my Bible (I did put that in a Ziploc bag) and began to read. It helped with my fear. God's word is cool like that. I tossed and turned and thought every noise was someone coming up on me, a tree coming down or a host of other things. It rained all night and I do mean all night, and the wind blew as well. I probably slept 30 minutes or maybe an hour, and then praise God, it was daylight. Now what?

Some of my thoughts on Day 1:

Day one was eye-opening to say the least. I felt frustration, anger, fear, resentment, embarrassment, joy, and conviction all in the first day. I will tell you this; I noticed people don't really notice what is going on around them. Most of the time, we are all in such a hurry with our lives when there are people in need all around us. I wanted to feel what they feel, but had no idea how overwhelming it would be. The end of that day brought knowledge to me that no book had ever done. I also thought that sometimes it's just easier to not know what is going on in the world around us because it takes away the obligation to do something. But that is not what I read in God's word. Those in need are His heart and who He talks about the most. We all need to just open our eyes — there are needs all around us that God wants to meet through us, but if we ignore the call, we miss so many blessings.

Day 2:

It is 6 a.m. at the start of day 2, and I had a rough night! Sound really carries in the woods, and it sounded like everything was right on top of me. I got out of the tent and gathered all my wet clothes and put them in my wet backpack. I had decided to go to the Laundromat and dry all my stuff including my bag. I headed that way. As I was coming out of the woods, a police officer was sitting in his car right where I came out, and I thought "Oh no, I am busted," but he didn't even look at me.

I kept walking and stopped by a local hotel. I went in and asked if I could get a cup of coffee and the man at the desk said yes and pointed me to the coffee. This had to be the best cup of coffee I have had in a long time. I then walked to the convenience store close by, and I decided to ask if I could use the restroom. (For those that know me, I have a thing about public restrooms, but I have a *bigger thing about going out in the woods!) They said I could use their facilities, so I did and I also washed up while I was in there. It was now 6:45 and the Laundromat didn't open until 7 a.m., so I sat out front and waited for them to open. I took $2 and put everything I had in the dryer and dried it. At the same time, I charged my phone up and looked at the newspaper. It was slow and not many people were there, so it was nice. Once everything was dry, I decided to go in their bathroom and put on my dry clothes and then dry the ones I had on. After I finally finished drying everything, I decided to start walking, and once again, it started to rain. I ran to an overhang of a local business so I could keep everything dry. It didn't rain long, so I got back to walking. I decided to figure out which church God wanted me to go to, so I started to pray. I walked and I was thinking, man I am hungry.*

I continued to walk and I felt the Lord lead me to a particular church. So, I headed that way, walking past other churches and watching families going into church together. I started to miss my family and wondered what it is like for those that are out there each day who don't have anyone to see these people with their families. I continued to walk and got to the church at 9:55. The service started at 10. God had confirmed this was the church where He wanted me. I went to the front door and the greeters were very friendly and pointed me to the door leading in to the worship room. I went in and it was dark, which was good. I sat on the back row and put my bag under my seat. The worship band was good, but I could not concentrate. I kept thinking how hungry I was, did I stink, what if that cop goes in and tears up my tent, where am I going to get more food, man I have to walk all the way back and a host of other thoughts.

To say it was hard to worship was an understatement. I actually left 30 minutes into the service. I began to walk again. I walked past other churches and saw people filing in. I really just wanted to be going to church with my family. I then stopped to rest a while. From walking with soggy socks and wet feet the day before, the bottoms of my feet were now one solid blister. I decided I would stop at another church and see if they offered any kind of food assistance. At the first church, I was met by a man at the door who asked me what I needed. I asked if they offered any kind of food assistance and he said, "No, we don't do that," and that was it. I walked away feeling kind of like an idiot. I came up on another church around 12:30 that had some cars in the parking lot and a sign out front that said "All welcome," so I thought maybe I could get some food here. I saw a man walking out and I said, "Excuse me sir" and he kept walking, and then I said again, "excuse me sir" and he looked toward me. I asked him, "Does your church offer food assistance to those in need?" He said, "I don't know. I haven't been going here long. Go ask someone inside." So I walked toward the door, and a couple came out carrying a large plate of food. They would not look at me. "Excuse me, does your church offer any kind of food assistance?" "We don't know. There are some people inside. "So I go inside, and there were two gentlemen inside the door. "Can we help you?" "I sure hope so. Do you offer any kind of food assistance?" "No, we haven't got that going yet, but maybe soon." I saw a bunch of people in the other room and a large table full of food. I guess they were having some kind dinner for their members. I walked away. This was probably the most humiliating, sad thing I had experienced in this journey so far. I was really mad to say the least, and I could see why the homeless I had met were so turned off by the church. I am not saying all churches are this way, but there should not be one like this. I believe you should not just give things out free without being intentional about getting to know them through the process but I also think you need to at least be nice.

I walked some more. I now know what Isaiah 58:7 means when it talks about the "poor wanderer." I was just wandering with no real purpose or plan. I was at a loss. Honestly, I was getting a little frustrated by now. I walked to a gas station, and they let me use their bathroom. I drank water from the bathroom sink for what seemed like forever. I went outside and sat down on the sidewalk, not really knowing what to do next. Well, I started walking and I came up on another church with a car in the lot. I thought to myself "Why bother?! They won't give you anything. Why try?" I guess that is how those who are homeless feel, too. I decided to go ahead and walk up there. When I did, I could tell the two ladies in the car did not want to roll down their window. A man came out from inside the church and the ladies rolled down the window. I asked them the same question I had asked the previous two churches and really expected the same answer, but to my surprise they said "Yes!" Praise God! They got the key to the food pantry and we went inside. They were very nice. They started to fill a bag for me with the typical canned vegetables that most churches give away: green beans, corn, and cranberry sauce. I told them I had no way to cook or open a can. They loaded my bag with pop tarts, canned beef stew (with a pop top), cereal and even gave me some soap and razors (I guess I looked pretty bad). They then offered to pray with me and to give me a ride to the Waterfront Rescue Mission. I told them thank you, but the food was enough. They were really nice and it made me very happy to see people actually doing what the church is supposed to do. When I got outside the door, I put all the food in my backpack so it was easier to carry and went on my way. God impressed on me that I should go back to this church and let them know what I was doing and donate toward their food ministry when this was all over. I started walking back to my tent, thinking the whole time about making sure my tent was OK. It was around 3 p.m. I got back to the tent around 4 and everything was good. That was a relief. It was starting to get cool, and I knew I was in for a long night. I broke open the beef stew and ate it. Yes, I ate it cold, and it was good! I started to put on layers of clothes. I stayed outside the tent for an hour or so, and the whole time I couldn't relax. I kept thinking someone was going to come walking up on me. At about 5, I got inside my tent and inside my sleeping bag so I wouldn't get too cold. Then, it hit me that I was going to be in there for the next 13 hours with nothing to do. I started to read my Bible. At this point, I felt God telling me this would be my last night as a homeless person, but I wanted to make sure it was Him and not me. As I read, He led me to Isaiah 58:7 "Is it not to share your food with the hungry and to provide the poor wanderer with shelter." I knew I was to pack up my stuff in the morning and He would lead me to someone in need of my tent, sleeping bag and the food I had. It was getting dark and cold outside, so I lay down. I remember thinking, "12 hours, 11 hours, 10 hours..." until daylight. I couldn't get comfortable, and I kept hearing all kinds of noises, thinking the worst of course. I prayed what seemed to be all night, but I did get a few hours of sleep and then it was morning. Thank you, God, for the daylight!

My Thoughts on Day 2:

Day 2 helped me begin to understand the daily struggles of those in need. I felt the frustration of humbling yourself to ask for help and not receiving it from where you feel you should. I felt the feeling of hopelessness and a lack of purpose that they must feel — what it's like to just be wandering through life.

I know most of you want to know what churches I stopped at, but I am not going to say because we must decide which church WE will be. I will say I went to three different denominations. We are each the church and it is up to us individually to make a difference. I know this, most of us have placed the homeless or those in need into two categories — either criminals or lazy. I see that it doesn't matter if they are good people; we have already cast judgment on them based on their situation instead of the person that God made them to be.

My 10-year-old daughter told me when I was getting ready to do this that I didn't have to be afraid. I asked her why not and she said, "Because you are the one they are going to be afraid of." I asked her why she thought that, and she said, "Because people are afraid of homeless people." I asked her why she thought people are afraid of homeless people, and she said, "Because they don't know them." I asked her if she was afraid of the homeless people we have met at the cafe, and she said, "No, because I got to know them."

We need to get to know people before we pass judgment on them. I understand we must be careful and not just give a person the keys to our home. I also know if we walk in the Spirit and allow God to lead us, He will show us what to do. When someone says all Christians are hypocrites, it's not fair to the Christian. When someone says all homeless are criminals or lazy that is not fair to them, either. Many times in the Bible, God says help the poor and needy. God just wants us to be willing to help anyone and He will bring those in our path that He wants us to help. We can't do everything, but we can do something. We just have to be willing. Join me today and ask God to show you a need and give you the ability to meet that need.

Day 3:

I got up this morning and still felt like I was supposed to pack up my tent, sleeping bag, and the food I had received from the church yesterday and that God would lead me to someone who needed it. After getting it all packed up, I headed out to the bus stop. I had $5 left, and I could buy an all-day bus ticket for $3. The bus wasn't there yet, so I waited. It came around 7, and my money was still wet, so it would not go into the machine. The driver did not have any dry money to swap with me, but a nice younger guy had some ones he traded with me. I really had no idea where I was going, but I knew this bus would at least get me to the mall, where all the other buses leave from. I got to the mall around 7:30 and waited on the next bus. I prayed and felt like I was supposed to go to the Tillman's Corner area. I got on that bus and was shocked to see all the people that use the bus to go to work. Think how hard it would be to time it so you weren't late to work. I met a lady named Joan who is homeless, and she rides *the bus all day long for $3. She doesn't really have anywhere to go, but it gets her out of the weather and she mostly sleeps. "I bet that is great when it is raining," I said. She nodded her head. She was nice, but painfully shy, so I didn't get much of her story. The bus takes you to the Walmart on Rangeline Road, so I got off the there. My feet were still killing me. The bottoms of both of my feet were covered in blisters. I started walking toward the Tillman's Corner area. I was walking across a parking lot, asking God to show me who needed the stuff I was to give away. I walked for about 30 minutes, and then I saw a man coming toward me. I felt in my spirit that he was the man who needed it. I walked up to him and asked if he knew anyone who needed a tent. Butch started to tear up. He said he and his wife had been sleeping on the ground in the woods, covering up with a tarp at night. I told him God wanted him to have this one, along with a sleeping bag and some food. Butch was a very hard looking man, but I could almost visibly see his hard exterior melt away and reveal a man who was hurting and in need. God used me to meet that need for him. I now knew for sure I had heard from God and it wasn't me just wanting to go home. Butch asked me if I wanted to meet his wife, so I walked back in the woods with him and met her. He showed me the spot where they had been staying, and he was very proud to show his wife the tent. She was excited, but you could tell she did not totally trust me. It was so awesome to see God meet the need of someone I didn't even know, and He let me* *be a part of it. They just wanted someone to care. It didn't matter who. I left them and went to McDonald's to get a cup of coffee and to charge my phone. I started walking back toward the woods where I had left Butch and his wife, and I met Jeffery. He was an older gentleman who had lost his job and had been out of work for a while and had really just given up on ever finding work again. We talked about how long he had been homeless and then got into a conversation about church and Jesus. He assured me that if it wasn't for Jesus, he couldn't make it out there, but he was feeling defeated.*

Then, a man named Roger walked up and began to talk to us. They told me that most of the people out in the streets are not bad people. They said there are some bad people out there, but they don't hang around with them. I saw some really neat qualities in these two guys that I wish I had sometimes.

I know a lot of people, including myself before I really started getting to know people in this position, would see these guys and think, "Bum! Why don't he get a job?!" but these guys are people — hurting, confused, struggling, people. I count it a blessing to have met these guys and hear about their stories and struggles. They seemed to open up to me because I was one of them, but really I think they would open up to anyone who seemed like they cared. It was an eye-opening experience, and I thanked God for leading me there. I decided I was going to walk back to the bus. It was now close to 11 a.m., and I could get on the bus and maybe go get a hot meal at 15 Place, a place for people to eat and get help downtown. I got on the bus and it took me to the mall, and then I had to get on another bus to go downtown. We got downtown around noon, and the drop-off was about 12 blocks from 15 Place, so I had to walk. It was Mardi gras, so there were many people downtown that day. I got to 15 Place, and they were closed. I then walked to the square downtown and asked a couple of homeless guys if anyone was feeding today, and they said the Salvation Army was at 3 p.m. I was hungry. I started to walk around looking for something to eat. I walked down Government Street, and there were parades going on. Everyone was having a blast. I had only been out there three days, and I missed my family so much. Watching all these people with their families made it even worse. As I walked, people on the floats threw things my way. A Moon Pie landed at my feet, and I picked it up so fast I just about hurt my back. I ate that thing so fast and then went looking for more. That was the best Moon Pie I had ever eaten! I probably ate eight Moon Pies, I walked and saw a vendor booth and went up to the man and asked him if he had some water and how much it was.

"This is donation only. We are trying to do what a local cafe does here and help people out," he said. I smiled and thought, "God you are so good!" He just kept giving me signs that I was right where He wanted me. I told the man at the booth I only had 15

cents. "Well, that's a donation," he said. I had to walk another 10 blocks to catch the bus because the bus was not coming all the way into town since it was Mardi gras. When I got to the bus stop it was 2 p.m., and I waited for the next bus. It never showed up, so I had to catch the bus going into the downtown bus station and then catch the bus back to the mall. We pulled up to the GM&O building as the mall bus was leaving, so I had to wait another hour. I got to the mall around 5 p.m. and then back out to the Providence Hospital bus stop at 5:30 p.m. I walked up to my car at the cafe at about 6 p.m. I put my backpack in and climbed inside my car. As I sat down, I began to weep. All that I had experienced, all I had felt, and all I had seen hit me all at once. It was a flood of emotions. I thought about how blessed I am, and I thought about all those I had met and thousands of others all over this country who do not have a place to go home to. I drove home feeling so overwhelmed at all I had learned and all God was teaching me through this experience.

My thoughts on day 3:

I learned that there are good people who are just in need of someone to show they care. I also learned that if we just get to know someone, we might find out they are not much different from us. Everyone has struggles. We don't all have the same ones, but we all struggle. We all want to belong and to be treated with respect, and just because we don't have a home doesn't take that desire away. I would like everyone who reads this to understand that all people are made in God's image, no matter where they live or what they do. God loves them, and He wants us to love them, too. Show your fellow humans respect, and treat them with the same respect you want to be treated with. We also need to be led more by the Spirit of God and not by our own spirit of fear when it comes to helping others. God will lead us to a need, and He will also give us the ability to meet that need if we would just ask Him. It breaks my heart when I think about all the blessings (like the one with Butch) that I miss because I let my fear, busyness, ignorance, and indifference lead me instead of God's spirit. I wonder how many times people cry out to God to meet a need and He puts it on someone's heart to meet that need, but they ignore it because they are too busy or too scared. It looks to the person in need like God doesn't care when it really isn't God that doesn't care, it's us. We as the church need to stop preaching about a loving, caring, God and start living like we believe it. People are tired of hearing about it. They want to see it, and it starts with us.

My homeless experience was one of the most life changing things I've ever done. It made me look at people differently. I know in my three days, I still didn't learn the full scope of what the homeless encounter or emotionally process on a daily basis because in the back of my mind, I knew I had a place to go when it was done. When I did go home I got in the shower and I will tell you it was the most amazing shower I have ever taken and sat in there for a long time and I will admit cried knowing that all those I met didn't have this luxury and I prayed God we need to get showers and Laundry to people in need of these services I saw how people could feel less than human when they live on the streets and do not have access to showers. Then if they are able to shower, they have to put back on the same smelly clothes they were wearing before. While I had seen military shower trailers or laundry trailers that big corporations would take to the site of a natural disaster, I had never seen one unit that could do both.

So we started the process of praying for and about a trailer that we could build that would house both shower rooms and a laundry facility. We wrote on a piece of paper what we thought would work and then for 1 year we prayed about how we could do this. We found a company that would build it and it would cost more, no way more than we had but we knew this was a need and that God would provide if it was something that He wanted. We reached out to some local businesses, churches, and families and raised the money to have the Clean Machine built. It was so cool how God provided these funds and even in the middle of it all things came up that had no other explanation but God. We had collected ½ the money needed and that is what we needed to get the process rolling so we ordered the trailer not really knowing where the other ½ would come from. The builder said it would take 6 weeks to complete. Over that 6 weeks we collected $6,000 more so we still needed $15,000. I received a call from the builder stating it would be another 2 weeks because the washers had been backordered. So over the next 12 days nothing came in and I received a call from the builder that the trailer was ready for pickup! Still $15,000 short we went to praying on day 13 we received a call from a donor and he asked how much we needed and I told him $15,000 and he said he would drop a check off the next day!! All I could think is WOW God is so awesome! I will admit I asked why the last minute provision but just as that thought came another thought came. If not last minute it wouldn't of been as cool of story.

The Clean Machine is a 22 foot trailer that has two bathrooms with a toilet, shower, sink, and mirror in each one, as well as three washing machines and three dryers. We can take it anywhere and wash clothes and provide showers for those in need. It is an awesome ministry tool. Over the years we have done thousands of loads of laundry and people have taken thousands of showers but the coolest thing is to see the way people go into the shower and the way they come out.

Do you have an idea that seems crazy or maybe it seems there is no way it could happen. I challenge you to put your doubt aside and move towards TRUST, FAITH and UNDERSTANDING in the one who makes all things possible.

As we go through this journey called life we will come up against things that seem impossible. But as we add the Lenses of God we will start to see that we were made to walk in the impossible you see the bible says in Luke 1:37 "Nothing is impossible WITH GOD!"

CHAPTER 4

(ACTION)

FAT AND HAPPY

In addition to the realization of the need for laundry and shower services that led to the idea for the Clean Machine, my homeless experience also caused me to realize how fat and lazy I had become. All that walking all over town and going without food was tough. My becoming a fat boy was a gradual thing; didn't happen overnight. When I was a young man, I wanted to be an athlete and when I asked my middle school coach what it would take for me to make the football team, he told me I needed to eat nutritious meals, run on a regular basis, do speed and agility drills, lift weights, and just get on the field and play. Along the way I realized all of the training was crucial to our team's success on the field, and the victories were what made the training all worth it. For most of my life, I have loved to exercise and play hard and have eaten somewhat healthy. I would take in good carbohydrates and proteins and then I would expend energy that would use those nutrients to burn fat and build muscle. Over time my life became busy with work, family, and church. I started to eat foods that were quick and easy, but not necessarily good for me. I would eat those foods in excess, but still go to the gym. As I saw the gains slowing, I got discouraged and frustrated that this was happening. I then started not going as much and would go out to eat instead. A donut with some coffee or loaded hash browns seemed like a great way to start my day. At first, I would feel physically ill after eating unhealthy meals, but my body began to crave sugary foods. I could eat some sugar cookies or a big juicy cheeseburger with some French fries and be stuffed, then go home and nap in my recliner. Before long my clothes started shrinking, or at least that's what I told myself, and the feeling I got from eating a high sugar diet made me feel good. I had become an emotional eater. I could go to a party and eat what everyone else was eating and be like everybody else. I didn't have to go to the gym any more. I could just live my life and not be bothered with thinking about my health. I guess you could say I had become Fat and happy. I was now happily married to Tara and I didn't have to impress anyone any longer, so why stress myself over eating healthy and going to the gym. While that attitude is messed up, it's a common trap that many married people fall into. We should always be striving to impress our spouse, they deserve it. My weight gain was so gradual that I didn't notice it much at all while it was happening. I know others saw it, but were too polite to say anything. After some time I realized what was happening, but I was so far in and it was too hard to stop. I tried to go to the gym and work off the donuts, but didn't see any quick results and therefore not much reason to keep going. It just took up more time in my day and made me feel sore and old. I would get discouraged and go back to my life revolving around food all in the name of fun. I just kept getting fatter and fatter, but I was always laughing and enjoying life so I didn't notice how unhealthy and out of shape I was. I had become the Fat and Happy person in the crowd, but deep inside I knew that was not who God intended to be. What harm was I causing anyone with my unhealthy lifestyle, though? I was happy, living for Jesus, and doing good things for others. I attended bible studies and even taught some. I didn't have time to do any real work on my health. I was too busy living for Jesus or so I thought.

Many people today go about life playing a game. They come across as having it all figured out. Every Facebook post, Instagram picture, and even their snapchat story make it seem like they have the perfect life and couldn't possibly be any happier than they are. Yet we are all constantly comparing ourselves with others and are any of us truly satisfied with ourselves? If it's not our weight, there are plenty of other things we obsess about. There are so many diet books, self-help books, and books about how to be a better you that we could probably read one every day for our whole lives and not read all of them. I've read quite a few of them myself. What it took for me to get back on track is to decide I was going to only take in what I needed to function and what was good for me. I only want to fill my world with things that could be used to help me persevere through life and gain victory over myself because really I was and am my own worst enemy.

As I mentioned before, each summer we bring in mission teams to work with us in our community for the week. We try to teach them the lessons God has been teaching us and as I told you we have a theme for the week. In 2013, our camp theme was, "I'm tired of being a Fat & Happy Christian." While I have told you my physical journey to becoming overweight, I also realized through my homeless experience that not only was I physically fat, but I was spiritually fat. Think about how I went from a healthy and fit guy to a man that was fat and happy because I consumed lots of calories, but never expended the energy required to burn those calories. Now think about your Christian walk. When you gave your life to Christ, you most likely said a prayer repeating after the pastor. Everyone congratulated you on making the best decision of your life and then proceeded to tell you all of the things you either needed to stop doing or could no longer do if you were going to be a Christian. Because of your genuine desire to learn and grown in your new faith, you probably questioned how you could instantly drop all of your bad habits. More than likely, your well meaning friends answer to your question was and would be today, for you to read the bible, pray, and go to church. Those three things are the fast food of Christianity. While reading your Bible, spending time in prayer, and fellowship with other believers are all essential parts of the Christian walk; they should always be done with the intention of knowing God and living a life that brings honor and glory to Him. They are not a cliché checklist of regulations for you to strive over. So, you join a bible study, Prayer group, and attend church every time the doors are open. If you had a key you would go more. You start to learn and memorize scripture. You go to men's bible studies, or women's bible studies, couples bible studies, breakfast bible studies, lunch bible studies, supper club studies, parent studies, new Christian studies, and more studies. You take in so much knowledge. You can sing the songs at church without the words on the screen and you only listen to K-Love on the radio. You can answer questions in Sunday school and drop your knowledge on those new to the faith. What I did and what I think happens to a lot of new believers is they consume knowledge and take in all the miraculous truths of Christianity, but then they don't do much to use what they have taken in. In the same way we need physical exercise; we also need spiritual exercise to keep us from getting spiritually fat. James 1:22 says *be doers of the word and not hearers only.*

We love to gather and fellowship together and as believers we should meet together to learn and encourage one another in our faith. The gatherings in and of themselves are not bad. Our time together at church and in our small groups is kind of like basic training in the military. We need the knowledge, the understanding, and the training. But we don't stay in training. We graduate and move on to serve in the armed forces and fight in battles or wars. We use the knowledge we have taken in and use it for what it prepared us for. The scripture found in Jeremiah 5:27-31 says *like a cage full of birds, their houses are full of deceit; therefore they have become rich; they gave grown fat and sleek. They know no bounds in deeds of evil; they judge not with justice the cause of the fatherless, to make it prosper; and they do not defend the rights of the needy. Shall I not punish them for these things? Declares the Lord and shall I not avenge myself on a nation such as this?" An appalling and horrible thing has happened in the land the prophets prophesy falsely, and the priests rule at their direction; my people love to have it so but what will you do when the end comes?*

WOW!! Just like us, they loved their gatherings and their knowledge, but did nothing with it. If all we do is study and get more head knowledge and have more meetings, but never do anything with our training to impact those in need, we become FAT and HAPPY. We are fat with knowledge and happy to just keep gathering with those like us. Jesus died for all; as in everyone. We are all made in His image. He didn't just die for those meeting in churches on Sundays. He died for EVERYONE! It's so much easier to just love each other and never really reach out to the needy around us, but God's word commands us to go into the world. It's time for us to get out of our spiritual recliners and get some godly exercise. We need to go into our communities and share God's word so that all may know Him and experience the joy and peace that only comes from knowing Jesus. We are called to help those suffering, not bang them over the head with knowledge, but coming alongside them and through a balance of mercy and justice, lead and disciple new believers the way Jesus intended for us to. We must learn from Him how to serve others, love others, and walk through life with others. Jesus is our model and example. This walk is not about having the most degrees, knowing the most bible verses, having perfect attendance at church, leading the most bible studies, or even how many people you got to say the prayer of salvation; it's about what you do with the gifts, talents, and knowledge that Jesus gives you to affect those around you. Now Go use what God gave you.

Salt and Light

At this early point in Ransom Ministries, one of the greatest blessings for us was being able to serve God as a family. God had also brought some friends along side of us that were looking for places to serve Him together. While I didn't give my life to Christ until I was twenty-nine years old, Tara grew up in church and as I mentioned earlier we were both good at doing the whole church scene. We taught Sunday school, sang in the choir, helped with Vacation Bible School, worked in the nursery, and were as involved as we could be, but to be effective salt and light; you can't always stay in the jar with the rest of the salt. Light is much more brilliant when it shines in the darkness. While assembling together as brothers and sisters in Christ to encourage each other in our faith is a joy and privilege of being in the family of God, that's not all we've been called to do. Our time together should be preparation for the ministry we will be doing when we are apart.

While not all of us are called to give up our secular jobs and start a non-profit, we are all called into full time ministry. In 2 Corinthians, the Bible tells us we are to no longer live for ourselves, but for Him who died and rose again on our behalf. We are all called to be Salt and Light as we live out our daily lives, so that others may see the power of Jesus working in and through us. We have also learned that we need to be just the right amount of salt and light let me explain. When a person is cooking and needs to add salt they don't want to add too much in at a time. You add a little and then taste it and then if needed add more. If you add to much salt to a dish it will not let the people eating it experience the dish for what it was meant to be. So when building relationships with others we must not overdo it if we add to much salt it will put a bad taste in their mouth and they will not want we have to offer. So too much salt causes the person to not like what we have to say but just the right amount lets them experience our real intent and that is to love them where they are. Now let's look at light and its purpose is to light our way whether that be a flashlight, a light in our house showing us what is in our way as we walk through the rooms or our car headlights. Let's touch on the car headlights there is nothing more annoying than someone driving around with their high beams on and it causing you to not see well. We flash our lights at them and probably flash other things at them as well. So when we are trying to live this life God has called us to the last thing others need it for us to blind them with the light we have. We just need to be a light unto the path that leads to God not a spot light shining in their eyes causing them to not see clearly what we really want them to see and that is the one true light and that is Jesus. I know I have also over salted and over shined in my walk with God thinking that was what I was supposed to do. But over the years I have learned to add salt when needed and to shine the light on the path leading to the light giver and it has taken so much pressure off this whole Christian walk thing and also prepared us for the next part of this journey

About one year after we opened the café, the local Habitat for Humanity approached us about partnering with them to build a Community Garden in Hillsdale, a mostly African refugee and low income family neighborhood. Habitat was donating a double lot, providing volunteers, and using grant funding to build phase one of the community gardens. They provided the water, as well. Our part was to maintain and expand the garden if and when needed which allowed us to begin building relationships in the Hillsdale neighborhood. God was teaching us that as a Christian non-profit, we should be partnering not only with local churches, but also with secular organizations to reach people. We found a common goal with Habitat, providing fresh vegetables to a community in need, and were able to use their resources to help reach others for Christ.

As the garden was being built, many of the neighborhood kids were interested in what we were doing and wanted to help. They also, enjoyed the fresh strawberries the garden provided. The goal of the garden was to provide fresh vegetables and fruit for us to use in the cafes and for the neighborhood families. While it was super challenging to communicate through the language barriers, we were able to form some beautiful relationships and pour into the lives of many of the children in the community.

Most of the people we met in Ransom Café were adults and many of them had years of bad choices and wrong beliefs that were difficult to overcome. Since we were called to help people realize their God-given abilities and to help them develop into who God intended them to be, why wait until they were adults? We needed to get some young people working with us, so we could teach them before they were so jaded by the troubles of the world. In the summer of 2012, Trinity United Methodist Church from Little Rock, Arkansas brought their youth to spend the week serving with us in Ransom Café, our Community Garden, and other partner ministries. The theme for our first mission team was Salt and Light. We wanted to use what we had learned about being Salt and Light and walk these young people through the process of using this Salt and Light in the biblical way to effect change in their communities.

We had a great week with the students, but a lot of people didn't understand why people from Little Rock would come to Mobile to do mission work. When most people think of going on a mission trip, they think about going to a foreign country for a week building things and taking them things they need and then coming home realizing how blessed we are as Americans and feeling good about how we had helped those poor foreign people. This trip was not that. It was more a chance to get them out of their normal environment where they have become numb to the needs around them and show them some simple, practical things they could in their community that is similar to theirs. So these camps were not about how much work we could get done or how hard we worked it was about building relationships and loving people where they are. We wrote on sidewalks with chalk, kicked soccer balls, made simple crafts, had water balloon fights, told bible stories, served meals, washed dishes and ate lunch with others. Our goal is for them to take home the things they've learned and for them to get involved in regularly volunteering with local nonprofits and secular organizations in their communities. At the core of everything we do is the desire to be salt, be light, and be Jesus to those around us.

We have continued doing camps and each year we have different themes such as #CoffeeBean, " I'm Tired of being a Fat and Happy Christian", " Camp Rio" and "Survivor we will discuss a few of these themes in later chapters. So as you read this book and go about your day think about this question. What am I doing to be Salt and Light to those around me?

So I can hear you asking but how do I do that? Well here is what we have seen that works BE YOURSELF WHERE YOU ARE! It really is that simple wherever you go on a daily basis Wal-Mart, gas station, school, work, or your home be a person that someone wants to be around call people by their names, ask people how they are doing and really mean it, just get to know people for who they are and where they are in their life not with the intention of getting them to believe like you but to really let them know you care even if they never believe the way you do. You see when we do things with other motives then loving them people see right through it we must love others because God loves them and it is His desire that they have a relationship with Him but even if they don't He still loves them and so should we. I will tell you some of the best places to be Salt and Light are in secular areas of your community so I believe we should not just volunteer with Christian organizations but also secular non-profits so we stop salting those that are already salty if you know what I mean. So today just GO BE YOU!!

An Egg, a Carrot, and a Coffee Bean Walk out of Church

Our culture has so many aspects pulling at us from every direction. Some things pull us to do right and some things pull us to do wrong. Many times we allow our decisions and therefore our lives to be affected by our circumstances or the things going on around us. Through that process we allow our culture to change us into what it wants us to be causing us to become someone other than who God intended us to be. I was speaking at a small church in Mountain Springs, Alabama when the lady shared this truth with the children using three unlikely items to illustrate this point. It so resonated with me, that it became the theme for our mission teams the next year.

There's an old expression that people use when they are in turmoil. They say they are in "hot water." Because our civilization is often a place of turbulence for our illustration we will say that pot of boiling hot water is our modern everyday culture. Now let's look at the various reactions that an egg, a carrot, and a coffee bean have when placed in hot water.

We will first look at an egg. Not only do eggs make a great breakfast, but they also can actually produce life if put in the right circumstances. However, if you put an egg in boiling water within ten minutes, it becomes hard. It's no longer capable of producing life and the egg's main purpose is lost. In the same way, as we go through tough times in our lives we can easily become hard hearted from the pain of disappointment, discouragement, divorce, or death.

The hurt from hard situations causes bitterness and resentment towards others and often times even towards God, thus paralyzing us with despair and hindering us from our God given purposes. Over the course of our lives we will go through many unfair obstacles. These things can either make us hard towards God and others or they can cause us to cry out to God and reach out for support from family or friends. While we mostly cannot control our culture, we can choose how we react to it. A biblical example of a man that allowed circumstances and greed to harden his heart to the things of God is Judas. He was the one that kept the money and was considered the treasurer for Jesus and the disciples so they must have trusted him. In John 12:1-8, we see Judas gets angry because a woman named Mary poured expensive perfume on Jesus' feet. Then Jesus told him to leave her alone and reprimanded him in front of everyone. This, I believe, hardened Judas toward Jesus and opened him up to be used by those trying to kill Jesus. When you hardened heart is not a good thing and can lead you down a path of destruction. Don't be an egg and let your heart become hard because of circumstances beyond your control or the actions of others.

Unlike eggs, carrots can be consumed raw, but they have very different reactions when boiled in hot water. A fresh carrot is crisp and full of nutrients. After being in the boiling hot water, a carrot becomes soft, gets mushy, and loses most of the nutrients it once had. You and me; we're busy. We just run around in our daily life getting kids to and from school and sports events while trying to be awesome at our full time job and sometimes we don't even realize that we are being affected by the things around us. Our convictions become blurred or soft and eventually the things that we once stood for really don't matter as much. When we first found Christ, we were so grateful for the sacrifice He made for us and we were eager to take a stand for our beliefs. Then over time the business of life catches up with us and the little frustrations eat away at our gratitude. At best, we are mushy. The biblical example of a carrot is Peter. Peter had a tough time holding true to his convictions in the heat of the moment. In John 13:37, we see Peter telling Jesus He would lay down his life for Him. Then we read a few more chapters and see this same man that once said he would fight for Jesus and even die for him, well let's just look at it.

Now Simon Peter was standing and warming himself. So they said to him. "You also are not one of the disciples, are you?" He denied it and said, "I am not." One of the servants of the high priest, a

relative of the man whose ear Peter had cut off, asked, "Did I not see you in the garden with him?" Peter again denied it, and at once the rooster crowed. John 18:25-27

When Peter experienced a little pressure, he became soft just like a carrot in hot water. Life is busy and distractions are all around us. We must be willing to keep believing and stand firm in our faith, no matter what other people think or what is going on around us. Don't be a carrot and become soft in your convictions.

The Coffee bean is the most magical little bean on the planet. We take this little bean roast it with fire and then grind it up and run the hot water through the ground up beans and we have an amazing liquid that affects everyone that drinks it in a powerful way. It can take a person from a dead sleep to Olympic sprinter in twenty ounces. Well maybe that's a little exaggeration, but it is some amazing stuff. I love to drink a good cup of coffee first thing in the morning. Even if you're not a coffee drinker, you probably like the smell of it. Its aroma catches attention and draws people in making them feel warm and cozy. Coffee is one of the few things that become stronger when it is ground finer. Did you know that coffee ground right before it is used has much more flavor than pre ground coffee? The grinding process makes it stronger and more flavorful. In Acts 9, Saul was traveling to Damascus to threaten to kill some disciples of the Lord that he didn't like. He felt they were a threat to his Jewish heritage and he wasn't going to just stand around while they spread lies. Along his journey, there was suddenly a bright light that flashed around him and he fell to the ground. Then he heard a voice ask him, "Why are you persecuting me?" He asked the voice who he was and was told it was Jesus and for him to go to the next city and he would be told what to do. The light had left him blinded and the men with him, who had also heard the voice, helped him to the city. I'd call that grinding. Well to make a long story shorter a man named Ananias was sent by the Lord to help him regain his physical sight and open his spiritual eyes. After giving his life to Jesus and being baptized, Saul went on to be one of the most powerful leaders and preachers of the gospel of Christ. Saul would now go by his Roman name, Paul, and God called him to minister to the Gentiles who no Jews associated with because they didn't believe God would love and accept them. Paul was a spiritual coffee bean. He did not let his culture or his surrounding affect his attitude and mission. In Acts 16:16-40, Paul and Silas were attacked and beaten with rods and after many blows, thrown in prison for healing a slave girl; more grinding. In verse 25 of Acts 16, Paul and Silas were praying and singing hymns of praise to God while the other prisoners were listening to them. They were beaten for their beliefs and their response was to sing praises to God. In turn God freed them and the jailer gave his life to Jesus. How many of us are imprisoned by our own self pity and doubt? Paul and Silas could have easily thought they it wasn't fair, or doubted that God really called them to that situation, but they chose to trust and to see how God would be glorified. They were steadfast and continued in their obedience and praise. Tara and I have been asked many times how we knew what God's will was for us. The Bible tells us in 1 Thessalonians 5:16-18, Rejoice always; pray without ceasing; in everything give thanks; for this is God's will for you in Christ Jesus. A dear friend of ours who battled cancer when he was here on earth, praised God for his cancer. While he hated Cancer and what it did to his body and how it destroyed people's physical temples, by his own testimony his cancer brought him into a closer walk with Christ that he may not have ever experienced. So he chose to say "nevertheless, I will praise Him". Coffee bean Christians are not affected by their culture. They are strong in their faith and trust God no matter what life throws at them. They choose to rejoice in affliction, to pray without ceasing, and to give thanks in all things. Be a coffee bean Christian and change your community for Christ.

Unfortunately, our churches today are filled with more eggs and carrots than coffee beans. Now when they are sitting in the building on Sunday mornings, they may look and act like coffee beans. But when they walk out the church doors and are faced with the reality of the world we live in, they become eggs or carrots. We must be a people that change our surroundings by the choices we make and by the way we live. Embrace the grinding. We are all a work in progress. God is making us finer and stronger so that we can use the gifts and talents He's given us to impact the world for Him.

Our mission team t-shirts were an ugly brown color with #coffeebean in white across the chest and the words "Mission Team" on the back. We got so many questions about those shirts. I'm not sure if people just didn't understand what coffee beans had to do with missions or if they just like coffee so much, they thought that might be a mission they could be part of. It's time for us to be different. If all we do is act like eggs or carrots, how we will ever change our culture and affect our communities? We must take what we learn and use it to transform the world around us. Once water is poured over ground up coffee beans, it's coffee. It's no longer water. It has been transformed and it can't go back to being just water. When you've given your life to Christ; you've been transformed. You can't go back to being who you were before. And why would you want to go back to being a stinky boiled egg or a mushy carrot when you can be coffee? Draw people in with your aroma of authenticity and joy. Be someone they can be comfortable sharing life with. Transform the world around you.

What are you going to be when you walk out of church? EGG, CARROT, or a COFFEE BEAN it's really up to you.

So as you build your TRUST, FAITH and UNDERSTANDING you must take ACTION or you will never put yourself in a position to see the power of God and the miracles that are all around you.

CHAPTER 5

(MERCY)

After a couple of summers of serving with the Clean Machine, we recognized how our opportunities to reach people had expanded with a portable unit. We now had Ransom Café's in five different churches and we were reaching people in different areas of our city. The next summer, our camp theme was "Search and Rescue," then "Live Your Passion" during the Rio Summer Olympics, and most recently "Survivor" because we've all survived something. God can use the things we've been through for His glory as we move from surviving to thriving. When we first started camps, the teams would arrive on Saturday night and we would immediately start serving on Sunday. We tried to give the groups a unique church experience and then we would serve the homeless with the Clean Machine or meals through a partner ministry. After four years of doing camp that way, God put it on our heart to take the first day allowing the teams to bond with us and with each other. And to spend time preparing them for the things they would do throughout the week. So we started having Sunday afternoons after attending church together as a time for fun and learning. We tried to prepare the team for some of the situations they may find themselves in and teach them what God has been teaching us about serving. Most recently God has strongly impressed on us to serve like Jesus did when he was on the earth; with a perfect balance of mercy and justice.

Mercy- that word means many different things to different people. A Judge might show mercy towards someone or a person might throw themselves at the mercy of the court. In the television sitcom Full House, Uncle Jesse would say “have mercy” when he saw something appealing to him. The Bible often interchanges the words mercy and love. Before I really knew what this Christian life was really about I thought mercy was for the weak. My mind would go to the old game I played as a kid where you would bend somebody’s finger backwards, twist their arm, or pinch them until they yelled out “Mercy!” So I saw the one doing the twisting as strong and the one yelling out for mercy as weak. When I started to learn about God and what He said about mercy I took on a distorted view of it. I saw God having mercy on people as Him letting them get away with things. I saw others who I thought of as mature Christians giving things away for free in the name of mercy or should I say in the name of Jesus. I learned from people that the way you impacted your community and got their attention was to have an event that boasted free hotdogs, bouncy houses, or a clothes giveaway. It didn't matter what you did, it just had to be free then you could get them in your playing field and share the salvation story. So free giveaways became the bait to catch fish and once caught they could be hung in the trophy case. I know I sound jaded towards those things but now that I have learned what Mercy really means; it has made me realize I had been doing things that were nowhere near what Jesus was trying to teach us when it came to serving others. I don't want to come across as saying we should throw all these things out. I just ask you to research the Bible and find the most effective ways to serve others that Jesus modeled for us. Mercy does have its place in the big picture.

Mercy, in order to see what Jesus meant this word to mean for us we need to look at the definition according to the bible. So I am going to throw some Hebrew and Greek at you because I know there are some bible scholars reading this and thus far I have been pretty basic redneck, so here goes. The Hebrew word for Mercy is RACHAM which means "to Love deeply", "to have compassion for others." The Greek word for Mercy is ELEEMON which means "Disposition to forgive or offer kindness in excess of what maybe expected or demanded." What happens when only mercy is shown to people in need? One thing that occurs when we show an excess of kindness is one way giving. One way giving is when a person comes in and has a need such as food. You give them what they need and send them on their way feeling pretty good about yourself because you helped someone in need. Then they come back with another need such as clothes and you give them what they need and send them on their way again feeling good about yourself and what you've done. You asked nothing in return for the food or clothes. It was just one way giving; you, either on your own or on behalf of your church or another organization, giving to them. So your relationship with that person is built solely on need and nothing more. When the need is met; the relationship is gone. *Toxic Charity by Robert Lupton* talks about the slippery slope that occurs with one way giving. Sometimes we don't even realize it's happening until we have slid all the way to the bottom of the hill. Here is the progression as laid out in that book:

- Give once it produces appreciation
- Give twice it produces anticipation
- Give three times it produces expectations

- Give four times it produces entitlement
- Give five times it produces dependency

What we see is as we give in a relationship built on need things start to get away from us. We start to resent that person and the person starts to resent us. One way giving hurts both the giver and the receiver. A personal example of this was when we first started Ransom Ministries we had a couple, I'll call them John and Jill, that lived in their car and had been doing so for some time. They came in Ransom Café for the first time and received their hot plate of food. They were nice and thanked the person that was volunteering that day. We saw John and Jill daily for about 3 months and each time they would eat. No one really talked to them about our model for the café and how we needed everyone to participate either through a financial donation or donating their time. Those are hard conversations to have and we knew they were in need. They lived in their car and you could see by their dirty clothes and their smell that were living in poverty. After a couple of months, something was changing in them and they became very demanding. They would complain about the menu or the food and were always asking for something more than a meal. One day when they came in, they said their battery in their car was dead and they didn't have the money to purchase a new one. I could have asked John to work for it, but that would have required me to spend time with him and I didn't have much time. I was trying to get a new ministry off the ground. So I took him to the auto parts store and bought him a battery. Well, a week later it was something else; some other part for the car. They kept coming into the café eating, demanding the staff to serve them and asking for extra things. Jill wanted her bread on her sandwich toasted because it was cold and John needed more sugar for his tea because it wasn't sweet enough. Demand after demand and zero appreciation. Soon we would see them coming and it would instantly put us in a bad mood because we knew they were either going to ask us for something or be rude about what we were giving them. While we were frustrated with John and Jill, we had created this problem by showing only Mercy. Our one way giving without having the hard conversations about everyone participating in the process hurt us and our volunteers, as well as John and Jill. We tried to fix their problems by what we thought they needed instead of by talking to them and listening to their real needs. Sometimes a conversation alone won't tell you everything they need some of those needs come out by what is not being said. I did eventually have a conversation with John and Jill about them participating in our mission by volunteering if they couldn't contribute financially. I told them they would need to come early so they could take a shower and clean up before being around food. They got mad at me for even suggesting such a thing and told me that it was not very Christian of me to require them to do something in exchange for their meals. We had really damaged them and it was too late. Notice I said *we.* We had served them and fed them and met some of their needs but we never really got to know them or really listened. We didn't show them we cared. What we did enabled them to stay where they were. We didn't help them get better.

Jesus gives us an example of mercy in John 6:1-15. A large crowd had been following Jesus so he asked Philip "Where are we to buy bread so that these people may eat?" Philip then said it would take a lot of money and still he didn't think it would be enough Jesus then said "have them sit down." So Jesus gave thanks over 5 loaves and two fish and then the disciples distributed the food. Jesus didn't require the people to fill out a form, show identification cards, or listen to a lesson. He didn't even ask them whether or not they believed in Him or if they wanted to say a prayer and accept them as their savior. He fed the hungry people a free meal. It sounds like Jesus was one-way giving, but the story doesn't end there. Many of us have heard the miracle of the loaves and fish, but haven't heard or paid attention to the rest of the story in the next chapter. In verses twenty-two through forty of John 6, Jesus has a tough conversation with the crowd. He knows the people have come looking for Him because they want another free meal and He confronts them. He goes on to tell them that they that believe in Him will never hunger or thirst again.

One way giving hurts both parties involved and Jesus didn't take part in it. It hurts the receiver by putting them in a position of entitlement and it hurts the giver by draining them of their compassion and causing them to feel frustrated and apathetic towards the taker. In many instances, the receiver already has a low self esteem and one way giving reinforces their negative thought patterns of themselves and distorts how the giver sees them as well.

One thing we believe when helping others is, "Never do for others what they can do for themselves." When helping others, it's better to have the hard conversations early in the process than later on down the road. It's better to sit down with the person day one, the first time you meet, and really listen to what they have to say and discern what their body language tells you. This is step one in building a relationship based on the person instead of on what they need or what we think they need. Assuming we know where a person is in life without really sitting down with them and listening to them is the one of the biggest mistakes we make. It's so much easier to just give a person with financial or material needs a bag of food, some clothes, a pair of shoes, or a hot meal and then send them on their way until next week. When we sit down and listen and take time to understand people, we could get involved in their mess and we might have to sacrifice some of our personal time for a new relationship. None of us have enough time in the day to do all of the things we *need* to get done and we just don't have time for anything but a monthly shift at the food pantry or clothes closet. Plus that doesn't stretch us too far out of our comfort zone. We can check "giving back" off of our "To Do List" and feel like we are doing our part serving without a huge time commitment. Again, I'm not against food pantries, clothes closets, soup kitchens, or other service ministries if they are not just giving away things for free, but inviting and encouraging those coming in to participate in the process while they get to know them and are intentional about building relationships with them. Doing this helps them feel better about themselves in the long run.

Before we start talking about *justice*, let's look at one more example of a *mercy* only ministry. Allow me to introduce you to my friend, Beth. She is getting ready to volunteer at one of our cafes for the first time. Some friends of hers told her about it and thought she would like it. Beth gets there the first day and she starts serving food to the guests and meets some really nice people. The church hosting this café doesn't exactly think the same way we do and don't want to ask the guests to donate time or money in return for the plate of food they serve them or for the clothes they give them they want to let that naturally happen. The do have a donation box available just in case someone wants to donate. Beth volunteers every week and each week she notices more and more people coming in. At first she thinks it's great to have so many people coming in and she feels good that she is able to do something to help the homeless in her community. Weeks went by and each time she was able to meet different people, but she noticed she saw a lot of the same people every week and she would have the same generic conversations with them. This really started to bother Beth and she wanted to ask them why they were there every week, but didn't feel it was her place to meddle in their business. More weeks went by and the crowd continued to grow. Beth would wait on tables each week and it was so busy that she only had time to take orders with a friendly smile and then she'd have to move on to the next person to get their order. Guests would shake their glasses at Beth when they were empty. They would send back food because the food was not hot enough and some even fussed at her if it took too long to get their food. The guests also started arguing with each other. They'd use foul language while yelling at each other and occasionally threaten violence. Beth would leave there each week exhausted and she started wondering if they are doing any good and actually helping people. One week when she just wasn't feeling it and didn't want to go, she thought what about those people that really need a meal and what about the commandments from Jesus to help those less fortunate than us. So she went even though she really didn't want to. Beth was on that downhill slope of one way giving where that café was treating a chronic problem like it's a crisis and it didn't take long for the Law of Diminishing Returns to take effect. You see I read in the book "Toxic charity that treating chronic needs as if they are a crisis causes dependency, deception and disempowerment". We see this quote at each of these levels in living color every day when we serve. Beth's story is not unique. It happens all over the world on a daily basis. It might not be a Café that feeds people; it could be a Food pantry, clothes closet, soup kitchen, school supply giveaway, bicycle giveaway, or a gospel outreach with free hot dogs and an outdoor movie. You always need free stuff to get people to come listen to the gospel or some other gimmick, don't you? Because it's easier to give away free stuff than it is to give of ourselves and our time to really listen to what's going on in a person's life, we often don't breakthrough into real relationship and fail to find the best way to help them get out of the cycle of poverty. I don't just mean financial or material poverty. Dropping a Christian track into a bag of food is a cowardly way to share the greatest act of love the world has ever known. We have to keep in mind the worst kind of poverty that we all have in common is our spiritual poverty; our need for a Savior.

The most logical way to fix the problem of one way giving is *justice*. Laying down the law, setting people straight, and letting them know who is in charge and exactly what is expected of them is what we need to do if they want to keep getting the services we provide. Right?

CHAPTER 6

(JUSTICE)

Justice; this word also means different things to different people. To some *Justice* is when someone has done wrong and they get what they deserve. To others *Justice* means the good guy got a win or something worked out fairly for two or more parties involved. So let's look at a couple definitions. First the Hebrew word for *justice* is TSEDEQ meaning something is right, ethically right or righteousness. The Greek word for *justice*, DIKAIOSYNE, is defined as Right or Fair. So Justice means what is right; what is normal; the way things are supposed to be; wholeness and restoration; conformity to truth, fact, or reason. So as we look at this word we see that *justice* sets things back to normal.

When I think about justice I think about being in a courtroom. No one talks without permission; the judge sits on his throne, I mean bench, and everyone rushes around to get the judge what he/she needs to hear the case. In the courtroom, defendants wait to be heard by the judge, but are often only allowed to answer questions about the accusations be made against them so a verdict can be rendered that greatly impacts their future. While this process is needed to keep order in our society, if that is all that happens do we get to the root of the problem. I'm thankful for the judges in our judicial systems that take the time to dig beyond the surface of issues and try to determine a fair consequence for perpetrator's offense and also what offenders need to move them in a positive direction with the hope of them not repeatedly breaking the law. In the context of ministry, justice is serving others through a system of rules and regulations. Justice alone seems cold and impersonal; not really concerned about relationships, but making sure everything is being done by the book.

Let me give you an example from my own experiences. When we first started Ransom, we had a grand idea that we would start a ministry that was "A hand up; not a hand out." Sounds like a good motto, but it was easier said than done. We came up with all kinds of rules to try to ensure that no one would take advantage of us. Patrons either needed to donate money or donate time and work for their meal *before* they ate. If people didn't sign up for a volunteer shift or contribute financially then we just wouldn't feed them if they came back. That was the rule. There were no exceptions. Everyone was held to the same standard. We even had signs made and posted in the cafe these regulations. When we started, it worked fine for the most part but as we got into it more, the rules seemed harder to enforce. Over time we would let people get by without contributing in some way until we would get frustrated with them and then we would slam the hammer of justice down and tell them we didn't appreciate being taken advantage of. We found out Justice alone does not work. It is cold and disconnected. We are on our throne with them hanging out beneath us waiting to hear the verdict as to whether or not we would bless them with our services. Justice by itself used to serve others looks like:

- A list of rules and regulations that must be adhered to
- Not giving at all because they're all lazy and need to get a job
- Giving with strings attached- makes good choices, listen to my sermon, jump through this hoop or I won't help you.

This seems pretty cut and dry and again we see all of these on a daily basis even in our cafes. I hope you understand that we have been in relational ministry for seven years and we don't have all the answers or think we have found the magic formula to serving, but we do know what has worked and not worked for us and we've studied the Bible to learn how to serve the best way possible.

Let's look at a time when justice only didn't work. This is probably one of the hardest stories for us to share with you. I am not naturally very merciful, but we are overly merciful when we are fatigued and it's out of convenience for us rather than empathy for who we are helping. Our harshest justice comes when we are fed up with the people we serve after we have been guilty of one way giving for a period of time. So we set up a bunch of rules and try to bring down justice in order to balance our overabundance of mercy. I like to say we don't do justice only very often, but I have seen mercy only turn into Justice and this story is a prime example of that.

It was a rainy summer day and we had the Clean Machine on site at one of our café locations. I was doing laundry for a guy named Shawn that was a regular and as I was pulling his clothes out of his bag to put in the washing machine, I come across a crack pipe in the pocket of his jeans. I was livid. I quickly take the pipe and the clothes and put them back in the bag and storm out the back of the trailer on a mission to find him. I found Shawn waiting in line to get inside the café for lunch. I dropped the bag in front of him and said I will not do your laundry if you are going to do drugs. Shawn tried to explain and I said no I don't want to hear it and I stormed off feeling pretty good about myself. I had stood my ground no questions asked and no excuses. Then Shawn came back the trailer and said that "I had no right to do that without hearing his side of the story" and I answered""I have heard excuse after excuse and I don't need to hear your side just move on". Then Shawn began to cuss me and call me names. I had probably embarrassed him by calling him out in front of all of those people, but I didn't care. The way he was acting just verified to me I had done the right thing and I was actually feeling pretty good about myself. Not only had I set Shawn straight, I had just shown a lot of those people that I was not going to be taken advantage of. A couple of months later, I started to see Shawn at the bus stop near my neighborhood. My first thoughts were there is that crack head, probably up to no good. Hard for me to admit and not at all the way Jesus would have me to respond, but it's the ugly truth. So anyway, for a couple of weeks I would see him almost every day waiting on the bus and these same thoughts would come in my head. Now fast forward 3 years, I am doing laundry with the Clean Machine at a café location again. We do things a little different than when we started. Instead of giving away essentials, we have a table full of socks, underwear, toothpaste, and toiletries for a suggested donation of 25 cents. I notice a man walking up to the table and I realize its Shawn. My first thought was, oh great this won't be good. He asks me how he could get these things on the table and I said we suggest a 25 cent donation per item and you can get as many as you want. He pulled out his money and said he wanted to get 8 pairs of socks. He called his wife to find out if she needed anything. He got off the phone with her and said I need these 4 pairs of underwear for my wife. He then looked at me and asked me if I remembered him. I said yes and he said to me, "See I don't do drugs. I use my money for good. I have a job and an apartment that I've lived in for several years. That crack pipe you found that day was not mine. I was letting someone going through a hard time live with me at my apartment then. It was his, but I had found it. So I had taken it that morning and I told him we needed to get him some help or he couldn't live with me anymore. After we talked, I stuck it in my pocket and I forgot it was there. That guy did get help and now he's is doing great." I was shocked and now I was the one embarrassed with the reality that I had treated him like a sub human and felt good about it. I did ask him to forgive me and he said "I did that years ago." Wow! Here I am this big bad Christian that runs a ministry to the needy and I was holding on to feelings of disgust for a man that I didn't give a chance to defend himself from my accusations 3 years later. Needless to say I was floored with guilt and I had to spend much time in prayer over this one. I asked God to forgive me and to help me not be so full of Justice that I forget to listen to Him and have mercy. I would also add that those times I saw Shawn waiting at the bus stop were missed opportunities God was giving me to make it right. I would like to say this is the only case were something like this has happened but that would be a lie. I'm getting better but I have a long way to go.

You see the struggle to balance it all is real each day we need to decide we don't have to be right or we don't have to make others right we just have to follow the examples God had given us and to walk in that. The thing is if we don't read in the bible the examples how can we do what He wants us to do. It is kind of like when we do things because that is the way we have seen others do things instead of consulting the experts on the subject. I think of the story of the lady that always cut off the ends of her roast before putting it in the pan. Those in the family asked her why she did that and she said " Momma always did that and her roasts were awesome" this made the others think so next time they saw

Momma they asked why she always cuts the ends off the roast before she cooked it? She said " because my pan was not big enough for the whole roast." You see many times we serve others because that is how we have seen others doing it instead of looking at the source and asking why and how we should do something.

So are you going to keep cutting the ends off the roast? Why don't you dig into the word of God and find out how He served others not just do it the way others have modeled it for you? Sometimes those we watch are just doing it how they were taught right, wrong or indifferent.

In the next chapter we are going to look at Balance and how God has laid out the process and the way to balance this serving others thing.

CHAPTER 7

(BALANCE)

As I have admitted, we've made a lot of mistakes along the way. Ministry is tough and sometimes it's hard to know if you're making a difference at all. We seemed to notice that we were having the same people in the cafes and the same people coming to wash their clothes. We felt like we were helping them survive, but God's plan is for us to thrive. So how could we help them move from surviving to thriving; that was the when God gave us the idea for Ransom ReProgram.

Ransom ReProgram is an 8-week job skills training program that seeks to provide participants with tools to help them overcome barriers to employment, helping them move out of dependency and into personal responsibility and a fulfilling career. ReProgram uses the Jobs for Life curriculum, an internationally-recognized job training program. Participants are paired with a mentor and are taught spiritual principles about work and relating to others. We first offered ReProgram in the fall of 2015.

We all like balance, but most of us need help finding it. We want just the right amount of sugar and cream in our coffee, just the right amount of smoke flavor in our BBQ, and the right amount of sugar in our tea. Before we share any stories of how a perfect balance of mercy and justice looks in our everyday life or ministry, we first need to look at the master of balance, Jesus. First let's look back at John 6:1-14, the same scripture we looked at in the last chapter, but this time we will look at the rest of the story.

After this Jesus went to the other side of the Sea of
Galilee, also called the Sea of Tiberius. 2 A large
crowd kept following him, because they saw the
signs that he was doing for the sick. 3 Jesus went up
the mountain and sat down there with his
disciples. 4 Now the Passover, the festival of the
Jews, was near. 5 When he looked up and saw a
large crowd coming toward him, Jesus said to Philip,
"Where are we to buy bread for these people to
eat?" 6 He said this to test him, for he himself knew
what he was going to do. 7 Philip answered him,
"Six months' wages would not buy enough bread
for each of them to get a little." 8 One of his
disciples, Andrew, Simon Peter's brother, said to
him, 9 "There is a boy here who has five barley
loaves and two fish. But what are they among so
many people?" 10 Jesus said "Make the people sit
down." Now there was a great deal of grass in the
place; so they sat down, about five thousand in

all. [11] ***Then Jesus took the loaves, and when he had given thanks, he distributed them to those who were seated; so also the fish, as much as they wanted.*** [12] ***When they were satisfied, he told his disciples, "Gather up the fragments left over, so that nothing may be lost."*** [13] ***So they gathered them up, and from the fragments of the five barley loaves, left by those who had eaten, they filled twelve baskets.*** [14] ***When the people saw the sign that he had done, they began to say, "This is indeed the prophet who is to come into the world."***

As we read these verses, we see two things Jesus is teaching his disciples about; faith and mercy. He fed these people without asking for anything in return and gave them as much as they wanted. Looks like *mercy.* He saw them in need of a meal and he gave it to them. He didn't ask for a form of identification, ask what their church affiliation was, and make them listen to a sermon first, or ask if they believed in Him. They were hungry and He fed them. Let's continue reading in John 6: 23-27:

[23] ***Then some boats from Tiberias came near the place where they had eaten the bread after the Lord had given thanks.*** [24] ***So when the crowd saw that neither Jesus nor his disciples were there, they themselves got into the boats and went to Capernaum looking for Jesus.***

[25] When they found him on the other side of the sea, they said to him, "Rabbi, when did you come here?" [26] Jesus answered them, "Very truly, I tell you, you are looking for me, not because you saw signs, but because you ate your fill of the loaves. [27] Do not work for the food that perishes, but for the food that endures for eternal life, which the Son of Man will give you. For it is on him that God the Father has set his seal."

Here we see the same crowd that Jesus fed was looking for Him. When they found him, He knew why they were there. They wanted another free meal and Jesus does what most of us are unwilling or don't feel comfortable doing and that's confronting them. He said to them, it's not me you seek; it's free food you are looking for and you're wasting your time. Let me show you your real purpose. What Jesus did by confronting them would be categorized as *Justice,* but we also see mercy in Him getting to the real issue at hand and making each person evaluate their motives while teaching them what they should be seeking. Now that we have looked at what the creator of Mercy and Justice did, let's see how this works in our lives and through some real life situations.

We had a young man named John who would come to use the Clean Machine at one of our locations each time we were there. He would stay to himself and not really talk to anyone and really didn't want anyone talking to him. Over time he opened up a little and would volunteer in the café while he waited for his clothes. I felt he would be a good fit for our Reprogram Job training program and one day I asked him if he would be interested in filling out an application. His response was "nobody would ever hire me for anything." So I let it go, but each time I saw him, I told him that he should never limit God and what He can do. I asked him to really consider being a part of our program and encouraged him that no matter what he had done in his past, it did not dictate who he is. As the weeks went on he told me he would like to try. He filled out an application and we met with him. His past was a big hurdle. I won't get into his whole story but because of some wrong choices he was homeless and living in the woods. Once we knew what he was up against, we weren't really sure we could help him. This was our first class of Ransom ReProgram and this was a huge roadblock to overcome. We prayed through it and decided this program was what he needed. It was for people exactly like John, so he became part of our first Reprogram class. During the class we talk a lot about being who God intends you to be and that His plan for us isn't determined by our past mistakes.

Through the eight week program, John started to open up and face some things he had hidden from others and even from himself. Over time he saw that he was a good person and that his past was not who he was. After graduating, John was our first student to get a job. He has had multiple raises and is one of his employer's best employees. It first took mercy to accept John where he was and to be his friend no matter what he had done so he was open to what God had for him. Then it took hard conversations to talk about these things and to walk through the process with him. We all learned together that most big hurdles are smaller when we attack them head on as a team. We are so proud of John and the man he has become. We pray that God continues to work in his life and are excited to see where his journey takes him.

Another situation similar to the one mentioned in the last chapter, illustrates better a balanced approach because it was handled differently. We were out serving with the Clean Machine at a regular location when a man named Jake who we had provided laundry services for about 3 months with no questions asked came to get his clothes washed. He would show up, usually high, and wasn't always the most appreciative for these services. As we got to know Jake, we saw a deeply wounded person who really didn't know how to function without drugs. One day while I was moving his laundry from the washer to the dryer, a crack pipe fell out of a pocket. At first I was upset with him and somewhat angry. This time instead of acting in my anger, I prayed and asked God to help me handle this situation in a way that would be pleasing to Him. I asked God to help me see Jake like He does. I realized this was just who Jake was now, but not who he truly wanted to be. I put his wet clothes in a bag and went up to him. I told him I couldn't do his laundry, but if he ever wanted to get help with his addiction, I would be glad to help him. Jake was furious with me. He called me names, cursed me out, and said I was not a real Christian. I told him I loved him and I would always be here if he ever needed help. He stormed off, but the next week he returned. It was very obvious that he was high, so I told him again that I loved him, but I wouldn't do his laundry. I reminded Jake when he wanted to get help, I would gladly help him. Again he cursed me out and called me names and said I wasn't a real Christian. About 3 months later, I saw Jake. This time he was coming across the parking lot with his head down. As he got closer, I could see tears in his eyes. He walked right up to me and said, "Matt I am tired of this life and want to get help". I told him to go inside the café and get a plate of food while I made some phone calls. The only in-patient rehabilitation center that would work with him, couldn't take him until the next week. I told Jake if he was serious about getting help, he needed to come back to this location of Ransom Café in a week. I prayed for him during that week even more than I normally did, but I really wasn't expecting him to show up. However, when we pulled up to the café a week later, there sat Jake with his bag of clothes packed and ready to go to the rehab center. Jake checked into rehab and became the person I knew he could be. He was a joy to be around and he now seemed to have hope. He went through 4 months of rehab and then asked if he could be part of our Reprogram class that would be starting in the next few months. I gave him an application and after the interview process, we decided he would be a good fit. Jake started the class and was doing great. He showed up each day of class, worked hard, and did a great job. I would like to say that he graduated and everything ended up great like it did for John, but that wasn't the case for Jake. He got impatient and frustrated that he couldn't provide for himself or his family. He began to hang with the same crowd he was running with before when he was a drug addict and things went downhill from there. He got back on drugs and most likely began dealing again because it was easy money and what he knew. We didn't see Jake for a few months, but then he came back to the Clean Machine one day and it absolutely broke my heart. He had done so well and worked so hard to try to better himself only to end up in the same place he was before. I had to have another hard conversation with him and told Him I loved him too much to watch him slowly kill himself with drugs. He was angry with me and left. I don't know what will become of Jake. I do know we have planted seeds of mercy and justice and I believe one day he will come back around. Unfortunately, we see this same sort of thing happen with so many of the people we try to help. While it's tough, we know we can't get discouraged when the outcomes aren't what we had hoped for. We have to continue to plant the seeds and trust God with the rest of the process. I will never stop praying for Jake and I believe one day, maybe not us, but someone will see the fruits of the seeds we planted.

The balance of mercy and justice looks different in all situations but it comes down to building genuine healthy relationships. As we go through the journey of serving others, we must be willing to move from mercy (relief) to justice (development). **We** will never pull someone out of their hopelessness, but we can be a vehicle **God** uses to pull them out and show them who they were created to be. Now that we see and understand the need for the balance of mercy and justice in building relationships, how do we accomplish it in the world we live in?

So as we move forward serving others through building relationships we must first TRUST adding to that FAITH, UNDERSTANDING, ACTION, MERCY, JUSTICE and then the last of all BALANCE this thought of serving others all comes down to Relationships. Everyone on this planet was made for Relationship and it is our job to intentionally seek out others to build these Relationships with.

CHAPTER 8

WHAT DO I DO NOW

These stories are great examples, but how do you and I know when and where to apply mercy and when to act on justice as you serve others? We have learned that God created us all to be in relationships with each other and relationships built on needs very seldom work. So, we need to consciously build relationships based on the person and not the need. One way to put that into practice is instead of doing things *for* them, do it *with* them. In the book *"When Helping Hurts," Steve Corbett and Brian Fikkert* break down the stages of giving;

- **Relief**- Urgent and temporary provision of emergency aid to reduce immediate suffering from a natural or manmade crisis
- **Rehabilitation**- Seeks to restore people and communities to the positive elements of their pre-crisis condition
- **Development**- Process of ongoing change that moves all the people involved, both the helpers and the helped, closer to being in rich relationship with God, self, others and community

A few common mistakes that we make are:

- Applying relief in situations in which rehabilitation or development is the appropriate intervention
- We are unable to shift from Crisis relief to the more complex work of Long-Term development
- Doing *For* rather than doing *With* those in need
- Try to give people what *we think they need* instead of what they really need

We all make these mistakes when serving even though we have the purest intentions. We want to see others do better and be happy. We often tend to think or feel like we have so much more than those we are trying to help and if they could just have what we have maybe they could be happy. Through much research of the Bible trying to see how Jesus served, I see that He always required an action when performing a miracle. One of the best examples of this happened by a pool of healing. I won't try to put it in my words; you can read in the book of John about a man who had been lame for 38 years.

***John 5:5-9** New International Version (NIV)*

5 One who was there had been an invalid for thirty-
eight years. 6 When Jesus saw him lying there and

learned that he had been in this condition for a long time, he asked him, "Do you want to get well?"

7 "Sir," the invalid replied, "I have no one to help me
into the pool when the water is stirred. While I am
trying to get in, someone else goes down ahead of
me."

8 Then Jesus said to him, "Get up! Pick up your mat
and walk." 9 At once the man was cured; he picked
up his mat and walked.

The day on which this took place was a Sabbath,

Can you believe Jesus asks the man if he wanted to be well? Doesn't that seem like a dumb question? The man had been a crippled for thirty-eight years, of course he wanted to be well! But instead of him responding how I think he would ("heck yeah!"), his response is to make excuses and blame others. He does not present himself as a person who wants to change and take responsibility for himself. Well, Jesus sees this and tells him to get up (justice). You see Jesus knew that this man had to see he could do it. He had to take ownership of his situation and get up. Many might think this a little harsh of Jesus. He could've picked the man up and put him in the pool or better yet just healed him where he was, but I think Jesus wanted the man to see that he could do it himself through the power of Christ. I don't know about you, but I see myself in this man. I often sit by the pool waiting for healing, for money to pay a bill, for a loved one to start making better choices, for that big break I need to be successful, and for many other things I think I need. I just sit there waiting. Have you ever been there before? Jesus is telling us to get up and do something. Don't just sit there and mope about all the things that are not fair, but get up and move. How many times have you heard someone say they were just waiting on God? We listen for God to say "Go," when we really should already be going and listening for Him to say, "Stop!" He already told us to go. The Great Commission commands us to go, but many times we are afraid. We are scared to get out of the comfort of our boat and start walking on that water. Aren't you thankful that Jesus sees us as who we could be; as whom He created us to be rather than who we see ourselves as? We need to see that! We have the power that raised Jesus from the dead living inside us. We are fearfully and wonderfully made. We can do all things through Christ who gives us strength. He gives us strength; not fear. Notice also how Jesus didn't point out this man's faults or try to force him to do what He wanted him to. Instead Jesus asked him what he wanted.

In the account of the Invalid, we glean a few great truths and build our serving practices from those;

- Never do for someone what they have (or could have) the capacity to do for themselves
- Limit one way giving to emergency situations
- Do *With* not *For*
- Empower others to do for themselves
- Don't serve out of Self Interest
- Listen closely to those you seek to help, especially to what is not being said

As we look at the different stages of giving and the way that Jesus served, it really simplifies the process of building relationships and serving others. We try to make things harder than they are by trying to invent a program, a formula, or a road map to serving. You see Jesus models not only in the story in John 5, but countless others how it's done. He goes about His day and as He sees people along the way, He asks questions and He listens to them. Jesus doesn't think through the process; He just moves about His day. And that's all we need to do is move about our day, always looking for those that need someone to listen. If we look and listen, we will see opportunities in every day to be Jesus to the world around us.

So now you may be saying this is all good information but what are some practical ways to do what I have read. First thing I would say is to start where you are. You say what does that mean? Start at home give practice on a daily basis listening to those around you then move out to your areas of influence and the places you go on a daily basis. Talk to your cashiers your barista's your well you get the picture get to know those around you as you go about your day. Then find a nonprofit I suggest finding a secular and Christian organization that is doing something you are passionate about and volunteer once a month if you don't know what your passion is just volunteer somewhere if you don't feel it move to another place but keep searching and I promise you will find it. As you serve be open to what God has for you and look for the needs around you I have seen ministries birthed out of volunteering and realizing a need is not being met. Most of all just be willing and seek God in prayer and He will show you the direction to go. Hey I never would of thought I would be here today serving others and writing a book!

CHAPTER 9

Practical Application

How to stay grounded on the Mission of serving others

The following is intended for intentionality in our spiritual Journey. This is not another law meant to be a spiritual burden, but a pursuit of Christ. Consider each of the following categories in daily, weekly, monthly, annual terms. Make sure that each goal is measurable, attainable, and as concrete as possible. Do not overwhelm yourself.

A. **Feed Yourself:** Feed your soul with God's Word? (Suggestions: Books, sermons, conferences, podcasts, Bible study, quiet time studies, etc).

Examples:

1. Read at least one spiritual book at all times
2. Listen to weekly podcast or radio program
3. Daily Devotional Reading Plan
4. Gospel of John
5. Psalms
6. Minor Prophets
7. Major Prophets
8. Read a Proverb a day

B. **Prayer**: How will I make room for God through prayer? (Suggestions: daily prayer time, praying on the hour, a monthly afternoon of prayer, a retreat of prayer?)

Examples:

A. Daily: Morning Prayer (6am) for personal life, Afternoon Prayer (1:30 p.m. post lunch) for church and ministry matters, keep up with my prayer board.

B. Twice a year take a half day away from office/house for prayer.

C. **Rest**: How will I rest my body, soul, and mind in order to properly engage God in my calling? (Suggestions: plan time away and actually be away, give yourself a bit of time each day, etc). Rest is for recovery, not sloth.

Examples:

A. Get away Daily (workout, golfing, coffee, walk around park)

B. Go away Monthly (stay in hotel one night, go to beach, go to hunting camp)

C. Get away Yearly (family trip, summer, spring break, holiday)

D. **Be Human:** What will I do to remember that I am a person, created by God, not an instrument or a thing only useful for working and tasks? How might I free myself to just enjoy something simple and material?

(Suggestions: Hobbies, exercise, cooking, or gardening, or being with friends. Where can you laugh?).

Examples:

A. Exercise (4 times/week),

B. Read four fiction novels, watch comedy, go to the movies.

C. Hang out with Wife/Kids/friends.

D. play Golf/hunt/ shop

E. **Community**: How can I pursue Christ through community? You are not on an individual journey. Christ is with you. Pursue community.

Examples:

A. Pursue Christ through weekly corporate worship and small group.

B. Meet with mentor once a quarter (list the dates)

C. Hang out with my friends and don't be uptight.

CHAPTER 10

Final Thoughts

In conclusion, serving others is not that complicated. Serving others is just about building relationships. Have you ever wondered why there are so many accounts in the Bible of Jesus eating with a wide variety of people? When you sit down with someone over a meal you put yourself on their level. Jesus sat and ate with those He wasn't supposed to in order to build relationships with them and let them know they had a friend in Him.

Over the years, we have seen some of the greatest miracles happen over a meal or a simple conversation. We have seen a Doctor's wife sitting and talking to an elderly woman who was lonely and just needed someone to talk to. We have seen a U.S. Senator sitting at a table, eating a meal, carrying on a normal conversation with a homeless couple that lived in their car. We watched as a young white teenage girl that was raised to believe black people were no good discovered that she wasn't better than them through sitting and sharing a meal with a black lady. We have experienced a man who thought the only way to make it through life was to be on welfare and food stamps meet a follower of Christ that was willing to walk with him through the process of obtaining employment, so he could support his family himself. We watched as a wealthy man that just found out his wife had cancer came to the café for lunch looking for someone to pray for him as he wept.

Relationships are the most important part of serving others. It's not about how many people you serve or how busy you are while you serve, it's about slowing down and listening to others and trusting the one who created all. We all have the same basic problems, just on different levels. No one is without problems. The bible tells us in this life we will have trouble, so why are we surprised when we have problems? The hardest part of serving is putting aside our predetermined ideas that make us like Martha in Luke 10.

***38** as Jesus and his disciples were on their way, he*
came to a village where a woman named
Martha opened her home to him. 39 She had a sister
called Mary, who sat at the Lord's feet listening to
what he said. 40 but Martha was distracted by all the
preparations that had to be made. She came to him
and asked, "Lord, don't you care that my sister has

left me to do the work by myself? Tell her to help me!"

[41] "Martha, Martha," the Lord answered, "you are worried and upset about many things, [42] but few things are needed—or indeed only one.[a] Mary has chosen what is better, and it will not be taken away from her."

Jesus tells Martha to slow down and choose to listen to the Lord. That's good advice for us today. Let's just slow down and listen so that we may be better used by God.

In review, we learned that we must TRUST the plan set before us to be all that God has called us to be. Then it takes FAITH to step out of the boat the first step is the hardest, and once we are walking on water, we must stay focused and obedient; we hope you saw how God is interested in every situation from the simplest to the most desperate. He is interested not only in the outcome but the journey. When we are in a situation that requires TRUST and FAITH, He is with us and usually sends someone else to walk with us through it. We learned through UNDERSTANDING we will see each person's struggles more clearly. We also saw that we can learn from the people we feel led to serve by listening to them and walking alongside them. We learn so much from sharing the pain of others and it can change our lives if we let it. We saw that we can either affect the culture around us or we can let our culture affect. We can get hard hearted when things get tough or people hurt us. We can get soft in what we believe when people question us or don't agree with us. We learned the grinding, the hurt, and the unanswered questions can make us stronger and allow us the opportunity to help others when they experience similar situations. We also talked about how we must exercise your faith in order to become who God created us to be. More knowledge doesn't do anybody any good unless we use it to serve and bring glory to Him who gave us the ability to have knowledge. We must take care of ourselves in order to be healthy and function the way God intended us to.

We saw that Mercy is a wonderful but potentially dangerous thing. We need to remember that mercy is a door not a destination. We also need remember that Mercy Alone hurts both the people we serve as well as ourselves and we need to know when to move to the next part of serving; development.

Then we looked at Justice alone as cold and impersonal. It causes a "me above you" mentality and could cause long term damage if applied by itself. Many people see Justice as a punishment for wrong, but really Justice is restoring things back to a healthy place. We talked about how balancing mercy and justice is hard and we must be intentional about serving the way Jesus modeled for us. We always need to look for opportunities to show mercy, but also intentionally move a situation towards development by holding each other accountable for our actions. We looked at some practical ways to achieve balance in the last chapter as well as what happens when we don't. This chapter showed us a perfect example of how Jesus helped others. Remember, we should not be sitting around waiting for Jesus to tell us to go. We should be going, listening for Jesus to tell us when to stop.

As we wrap up, I'd like to share one more story with you. There once was a man who was so far from God, he truly didn't think God existed. He didn't care to know much about Christ. After an injury ended his college football career, He went about life finding work and making a living. He was single, but found out he was going to be a dad. His first thoughts were; I can't be a dad! I don't know how. Then that baby girl was born and it changed his life forever. Not only did he become a father and a husband, but he also had a transformative encounter with Jesus and that put him on a path he never could've imagined. His family of three tried to live for Jesus and got involved in the church where their daughter was in daycare. Before long they were blessed with another little girl. WOW! The man thought God must really trust us to give us these precious gifts of life. A couple of years went by and they learned that girl number three would be born in May of 2002. But then his life took an unexpected turn and life as he knew it came crashing down. The man was angry and deeply hurt. He blamed God for this and didn't understand how He would have allowed this to happen. He wouldn't talk to God for a long time. He did his best to go about his life with things were crashing down around him. After the baby was born, he would have his daughters every weekend. He did the best he could to move forward for his girls. They spent their weekends watching movies, going swimming, having sleepovers with friends. The Lord in His mercy sent the man a woman that to this day he says saved his life, but at that time he was still not on speaking terms with God. He married her, adopted the daughter she had, and they had a daughter together. God had trusted him with 5 girls. Then things changed and it made it very difficult for him to maintain a relationship with 3 of the 5 gifts. They were growing and the traveling back in forth and the turmoil his girls were suffering broke the man's heart. He realized that if he continued to force the girls to have a relationship with him, they would hate him forever. He was hopeful that if he let them go for now, he would free them from the turmoil of a broken family and preserve their future relationship. The man was still mad at God. He was so frustrated and had got to the point where he would vent to God, but not really listen. Time went on and when the man started listening, God showed him the things that happened were not all His fault. God has given us all free will and these unfair things that had happened were the result of human decision. The Lord told him to just keep trusting and He would work all of it for good. (Romans 8:28) and ONE DAY He would restore what had been torn apart. The man decided that day that he would trust no matter what. Days went by; months went by, and then years. The man had not seen of talked to his daughters, but the man stayed true to his promise to trust God and hold on to the promise of ONE DAY. Some days he didn't want to trust and it was really hard. He wanted to give up or try to make something happen, but he chose to trust. Over the years, others around him tried to get him to push the situation, but he knew that was not the plan. He just needed to trust. The man went about life loving God and others and the relationships he did have were growing stronger. Many days he would cry out to God and ask "Why?" "When?," and "How come?" The answer was always the same; "ONE DAY". You see God is always working behind the scene and each thing that goes on is part of His plan.

Well, I would like to tell you that this situation has been resolved and that his relationship with his daughter's has been restored, but the story is still being written. The man found out some horrible things had happened to his daughters and he blamed himself and was angry all over again he questions God every day. Why? How come? Why did you let that happen? and the answer is always the same ONE DAY! God has given him a few "sneak peaks" of what is to come, but for now he is just moving forward and trusting Him. He holds firmly onto the hope he has in Jesus and listen for God to guide him along the way. One thing is for sure, he knows ONE DAY, God's plan will be unfolded before our eyes and what a great day that will be! You see the promise of ONE DAY is for all of us as long as we don't lose hope and Trust by Faith that His plan will unfold before our eyes in His perfect timing.

We have shared so much with you and hope you have seen that we don't have all the answers, but God does. We all need to daily focus on hearing Him and obeying His call for us to be in relationship with others. We appreciate you coming on this journey with us and we hope it has given you a fresh perspective on serving and inspired you to serve others. We hope the stories we shared encouraged you and will be a resource to you as you serve. Most of all we pray that you will look at those in need differently and that you will embrace your role in serving them. So as we conclude, we want to remind you don't be an Egg, or a Carrot. Don't be a Fat Christian, a mercy only, or justice only Christian. Change the world around you by being a Coffee bean Christian that puts into practice the things they've learned and serves with a balance of mercy and justice

Tips for better volunteering

It's better to do something small and realistic on a regular basis than make a large commitment you can't fulfill. It's also better to do something small than to do nothing at all. Check out the volunteer opportunities below to see the ways you can be involved.

Remember that helping people requires relationships. We so often make the mistake of believing poverty means people need money or things, but most people who find themselves in poverty get there by not having a support system. To truly help those in need rise out of poverty, donate yourself, not just your stuff.

If time to build relationships with those in need is not a resource youhave, serve in ways that make it easier for those who do. Sometimes an organization's greatest needs require unglamorous work that no one thinks of signing up to do: organizing storage spaces, cleaning offices, performing computer maintenance, filing paperwork, fundraising and more. Contact the organization you want to serve and ask them what no one on their staff has time to do. This is a great way to serve one time and really make a difference.

If you can volunteer regularly, spend some time just listening and learning, even if you have valuable experience and ideas to offer. Imagine starting a new job and immediately flooding your coworkers with ways they should do everything differently. Overwhelming! Instead, learn how things are currently done, and after trust and understanding are mutually established, begin making suggestions.

Donate money. Donate resources. Raise funds and awareness. Some people are called to give their time, and some are called to give money (what we find is that people usually start with one and it eventually leads to the other). If you're a high-powered executive who works 80 hours a week, you can't make time to volunteer on a regular basis. But you can provide much needed funding to make an organization's work possible. If you're a busy stay-at-home mom, you can't bring your two under two to volunteer, and you may not have the monetary resources to donate, but you could have your friends and family collect needed supplies. Others have the valuable gift of fundraising! Use your connections and networks to raise awareness for the organization you love to generate sustainable sources of funding and volunteers.

Questions to ask when wanting to serve others.

- Who in my home needs me?
- What friend do I need to live my faith in front of?
- Where in my everyday life do I see people that just need to be encouraged in order to hold on to the promise of ONE DAY?
- Who in my community does things for others that I am passionate about?
- How can I get involved with them?

Things to think about when Serving

- Serving others is not complicated it's just about building relationships.
- Relationships is the best way to live out the Gospel.

- Each Day ask yourself. What did I learn today? What benefit will it bring to my life? How can I implement it in my daily life?
- This is as easy as living your life in front of others.

Ransom
·MINISTRIES·

Po Box 851854

Mobile AL 36685

www.ransomministries.com

info@ransomministries.com

Ransom Ministries was founded in October 2010 by Matt and Tara Armbruster after they attended a Bible study urging Christians to stop playing church and start living a life of true faith and dependence on God.

The Armbrusters asked God to show them how they could use the gifts He had given them to bring glory to Him. God gave Matt the idea of a cafe where anyone could get a hot meal and pay whatever they could afford. Tara received the word "ransom" and the scripture Matthew 20:28. When they began to dissect this verse, they discovered the Greek word that is translated "to serve" actually meant "one that waits on tables," and "ransom" meant "to liberate many from misery."

Since 2010, Ransom Ministries has planted seven Ransom Cafe locations, two of which have taken on their own responsibilities. A portable laundry and shower trailer called the Clean Machine, summer mission teams, the Ransom on the Road food truck and Ransom ReProgram, a job skills training course that helps participants move out of dependency and into fulfilling career